Discard

Scott O'Dell

WHO
WROTE
THAT?

WHO WROTE THAT?

Scott O'Dell

Hal Marcovitz

Foreword by
Kyle Zimmer

CHELSEA HOUSE
PUBLISHERS
An imprint of Infobase Publishing

Scott O'Dell

Chelsea House
An imprint of Infobase Publishing
132 West 31st Street
New York NY 10001

Library of Congress Cataloging-in-Publication Data
Marcovitz, Hal.
  Scott O'Dell / Hal Marcovitz.
     p. cm. — (Who wrote that?)
  Includes bibliographical references and index.
  ISBN-13: 978-0-7910-9526-3 (acid-free paper)
  ISBN-10: 0-7910-9526-6 (acid-free paper) 1. O'Dell, Scott, 1898-1989—
Juvenile literature. 2. Authors, American--20th century--Biography—Juvenile literature. 3. Young adult fiction—Authorship—Juvenile literature. 4. Historical fiction—Authorship—Juvenile literature. 5. Children's stories—Authorship--Juvenile literature. I. Title. II. Series.
  PS3529.D434Z77 2007
  813'.54—dc22
  [B]   2007019577

Text design by Keith Trego and Erika Arroyo
Cover design by Joo Young An

Printed in the United States of America

Bang EJB 10 9 8 7 6 5 4 3 2 1

This book is printed on acid-free paper.

Table of Contents

FOREWORD BY
KYLE ZIMMER
PRESIDENT, FIRST BOOK

HUMANITY IS POWERED by stories. From our earliest days as thinking beings, we employed every available tool to tell each other stories. We danced, drew pictures on the walls of our caves, spoke, and sang. All of this extraordinary effort was designed to entertain, recount the news of the day, explain natural occurrences—and then gradually to build religious and cultural traditions and establish the common bonds and continuity that eventually formed civilizations. Stories are the most powerful force in the universe; they are the primary element that has distinguished our evolutionary path.

Our love of the story has not diminished with time. Enormous segments of societies are devoted to the art of storytelling. Book sales in the United States alone topped $26 billion last year; movie studios spend fortunes to create and promote stories; and the news industry is more pervasive in its presence than ever before.

There is no mystery to our fascination. Great stories are magic. They can introduce us to new cultures or remind us of the nobility and failures of our own; inspire us to greatness or scare us to death; but above all, stories provide human insight on a level that is unavailable through any other source. In fact, stories connect each of us to the rest of humanity not just in our own time, but also throughout history.

This special magic of books is the greatest treasure that we can hand down from generation to generation. In fact, that spark in a child that comes from books became the motivation for the creation of my organization, First Book, a national literacy program with a simple mission: to provide new books to the most disadvantaged children. First Book has been at work in hundreds of communities for over a decade. Every year, children in need receive millions of books through our organization, and millions more are provided through dedicated literacy institutions across the United States and around the world. In addition, groups of people dedicate themselves tirelessly to working with children to share reading and stories in every imaginable setting from schools to the streets. Of course, this Herculean effort serves many important goals. Literacy translates to productivity and employability in life and many other valid and even essential elements. But at the heart of this movement are people who love stories, love to read, and want desperately to ensure that no one misses the wonderful possibilities that reading provides.

When thinking about the importance of books, there is an overwhelming urge to cite the literary devotion of great minds. Some have written of the magnitude of the importance of literature. Amy Lowell, an American poet, captured the concept when she said, "Books are more than books. They are the life, the very heart and core of ages past, the reason why men lived and worked and died, the essence and quintessence of their lives." Others have spoken of their personal obsession with books, as in Thomas Jefferson's simple statement: "I live for books." But more compelling, perhaps, is the almost instinctive excitement in children for books and stories.

Throughout my years at First Book, I have heard truly extraordinary stories about the power of books in the lives of children. In one case, a homeless child, who had been bounced from one location to another, later resurfaced— and the only possession that he had fought to keep was the book he was given as part of a First Book distribution months earlier. More recently, I met a child who, upon receiving the book he wanted, flashed a big smile and said, "This is my big chance!" These snapshots reveal the true power of books and stories to give hope and change lives.

As these children grow up and continue to develop their love of reading, they will owe a profound debt to those volunteers who reached out to them—a debt that they may repay by reaching out to spark the next generation of readers. But there is a greater debt owed by all of us—a debt to the storytellers, the authors, who have bound us together, inspired our leaders, fueled our civilizations, and helped us put our children to sleep with their heads full of images and ideas.

WHO WROTE THAT? is a series of books dedicated to introducing us to a few of these incredible individuals. While we have almost always honored stories, we have not uniformly honored storytellers. In fact, some of the most important authors have toiled in complete obscurity throughout their lives or have been openly persecuted for the uncomfortable truths that they have laid before us. When confronted with the magnitude of their written work, we can forget that writers are people. They struggle through the same daily indignities and dental appointments, and they experience the intense joy and bottomless despair that many of us do. Yet, somehow they rise above it all to weave a powerful thread that connects us all. It is a rare honor to have the opportunity that these books provide to share the lives of these extraordinary people. Enjoy.

Scott O'Dell (above) is most famous for his book Island of the Blue Dol-phins, *though he wrote a total of 27 books for young people. His books cov-ered a wide range of topics, from historical to contemporary.*

1

The Lone Woman of San Nicolas

SAN NICOLAS ISLAND is little more than a barren patch of volcanic rock that rises out of the Pacific Ocean about 80 miles (128 kilometers) off the coast of southern California. The island measures a mere 6 miles (9.6 kilometers) long and 3 miles (4.8 kilometers) wide. It is hard to imagine anyone living there alone and yet, more than 150 years ago, a young girl known as Juana Maria managed to survive for 18 years on San Nicolas.

Scott O'Dell, who grew up along the southern California coast, learned about the plight of Juana Maria in the 1920s. A writer who was fascinated by history, O'Dell wanted to tell the story of the "Lone Woman of San Nicolas Island." He was also interested in San Nicolas Island, which is one of the eight Channel Islands.

In 1980, the U.S. Congress declared the Channel Islands a national park. Formed about 14 million years ago by volcanic activity in the Pacific, all of the islands are similar to San Nicolas: rocky, forbidding, windswept, and wild. Later, O'Dell said that San Nicolas Island was probably very similar to Dead Man's Island, a tiny rocky island near San Pedro, California, where O'Dell had lived for a time as a boy. When he was very young, O'Dell played near Dead Man's Island. O'Dell and his friends would float atop logs, using them as rafts to hunt octopuses, which the coastal people called devilfish. Recalling the story he had decided to write about Juana Maria, he said that it

> came from the memory of my years at San Pedro and Dead Man's Island, when, with other boys my age, I voyaged out on summer mornings in search of adventure. One day we left the landlocked world and went to sea, each of us on separate logs. They were twelve feet long or longer, rough with splinters, and covered with tar. But to each of us young Magellans, they were proud canoes, dugouts fashioned by ax and fire, graceful, fierce-prowed—equal to any storm.
>
> We freed them from the deep-water slips where they waited for the sawmill. Paddling with our hands, we set to sea—to the breakwater and even to Portuguese Bend. We returned hours later, having circumnavigated the watery world. Some mornings, in sun or rain, we searched for devilfish among the sea-washed rocks off Dead Man's Island.[1]

When O'Dell decided to write the story of Juana Maria's adventures on San Nicolas Island, he discovered that very little was actually known about how the young woman had

The Santa Barbara mission was established in 1786 by Spanish Fran-ciscan missionaries. Juana Maria, who inspired the character of Karana in Island of the Blue Dolphins, *lived here after her rescue in 1850. The current church (above) was built in 1820.*

survived the ordeal. George Nidever, a sea otter hunter who found Juana Maria on the island in 1853, discovered her living alone in a hut made of whalebones. Her skirt was made out of the feathers of the cormorant, a green sea bird found among the coastlines and islands of the Pacific. She spoke a language that no one understood. The woman was an Indian, but no other members of her tribe remained. Evidently, the tribe had left the island aboard a ship in 1835, but Juana Maria had been mysteriously left behind.

Even Juana Maria's name was a mystery. The Santa Barbara Mission in California, where she lived after she was rescued, decided to call her Juana Maria. No one knew her true name, and she was unable to make anyone at the mission understand her story. Only Father Gonzalez was able to communicate with Juana Maria, and he learned only a few facts. The most important one was that her younger brother was left behind with her, but he was killed by wild dogs on the island. Sadly, seven weeks after arriving at the mission, Juana Maria became sick and died. She had not been exposed to many kinds of disease while living on San Nicolas, so she had never built up immunity to common germs. Juana Maria is buried on the mission grounds.

CAROLINA'S RED SKIRT

In his story, O'Dell renamed the castaway "Karana" and based the character on the personality of a young girl he had known years before in Mexico. The girl, a Tarascan Indian named Carolina, was a maid who worked for O'Dell and his wife while they spent a summer in a quinta, or country house. He recalled:

> Carolina, the Tarascan girl of sixteen, who lived on the shores of Lake Patzcuaro in central Mexico . . . was one of nine children, the oldest daughter of Pedro Flores, who took care of the small *quinta* my wife and I had rented for the summer.
>
> Carolina, when she first came to work for us, wore a red skirt of closely woven wool. As a bride her mother had received the gift of sixty yards of this red cloth from her betrothed, a

Above is an aerial photograph of San Nicolas Island as it looks today. Largely uninhabited after the Nicoleños were evacuated in the early nineteenth century, the island now serves as a weapons testing and training facility for the U.S. Navy.

custom of the Tarascans. With it, by winding it around and around her waist, she made a skirt. At night she used it as a blanket for herself and her husband, and later for their children, against the fierce cold of the mountains. For each girl child she cut lengths of the cloth and this in turn became a skirt. The red skirt, the *falda roja*, which Carolina wore, came to her in this fashion. She wore it proudly, as a shield against the world, in the way Karana wore the skirt of cormorant feathers. The two girls are much alike."[2]

O'Dell titled the book *Island of the Blue Dolphins*, and created a fictional story as he retold real-life events. This began his career as a writer of historical fiction for children. Since no one knew very much about Juana Maria and her story, O'Dell found it necessary to fill in many of the missing parts on his own. For example, he named Karana's home the Island of the Blue Dolphins because Karana believes the island is shaped like a dolphin. In the story, Karana says:

If you were standing on one of the hills that rise in the middle of it, you would think that it looked like a fish. Like a dolphin lying on its side, with its tail pointing to the sunset, and its fins making reefs and the rocky ledges along the shore. Whether someone did stand there on the low hills in the days when the earth was new and, because of its shape, called it the Island of the Blue Dolphins, I do not know. Many dolphins live in our seas and it may be from them that the name came. But one way or the other, this is what the island was called. (*Island of the Blue Dolphins,* pp. 16–17)

Island of the Blue Dolphins was published in 1960. It was the first story O'Dell wrote for young readers, and it was a critical success. Indeed, the book would quickly find its place among the most important novels written for young readers. In the *Dictionary of Literary Biography*, book critic Malcolm Usrey wrote:

Island of the Blue Dolphins has few equals in children's literature. The novel attests to the skills and talents of O'Dell as a writer of historical fiction. He has woven a suspenseful tale

Did you know...

Spanish explorer Sebastián Vizcaíno sighted San Nicolas Island on December 6, 1602. He named the island after Saint Nicholas because December 6 is St. Nicholas's Feast Day, a festive holiday that is celebrated in Europe, much like Christmas.

San Nicolas is one of the eight Channel Islands located off the coast of California. In 1980, Congress designated most of the islands a national park. The National Park Service acquired the final island, Santa Cruz, in 1997. Six miles (9.6 kilometers) of ocean surrounding each island is protected, which means that the territory is off-limits to fishermen, oil drilling, and other commercial enterprises.

Channel Islands National Park is open to visitors. Many hardy campers who seek adventure pitch their tents on the islands. In 1999, *New York Times* editor Barbara Strauch visited the islands and reported that her boat was accompanied by dozens of dolphins as it approached Santa Cruz. This was similar to the way Scott O'Dell described the dolphins who accompanied Karana's canoe whenever she ventured off the San Nicolas shore.

Strauch wrote, "My daughter, Meryl, 11, and I were near the bow when she spotted them—off to the left—not one, not two, but dozens of dolphins, their sleek, gray-black bodies leaping out of the green ocean. They jumped in pairs, in unison, playing in the wake. One cruised alongside the boat in the full force of the foam—getting a massage? Just showing off? Others pirouetted only feet away, so close and so many it was thrilling."*

---

* Barbara Strauch, "Camping on an Island of Menacing Mice," *New York Times* (October 3, 1999): p. 8.

around one of the most appealing of all subjects, survival of a man or woman against the odds of nature in an extremely primitive environment. . . . *Island of the Blue Dolphins* is surely O'Dell's masterpiece and one of a half dozen or so great historical novels for children by an American writer in the past two or three decades."[3]

Young readers continue to embrace the story, even decades after it was first published. The book has sold millions of copies; in fact, each year, about 170,000 new copies are sold to readers who are just discovering Karana's story. According to *Publisher's Weekly*, the trade journal of the book publishing industry, paperback sales of $6.6 million place the book sixth on the all-time list of paperback sales of books for young readers. Even more important, shortly after publication of the book, the American Library Association awarded O'Dell the Newbery Medal, which is considered the most prestigious award for children's literature in America. *Island of the Blue Dolphins* helped launch O'Dell's career as an author of juvenile fiction.

O'Dell would go on to write another 25 novels over the next 29 years, most of them in the genre of historical fiction. In 1972, the queen of Denmark presented O'Dell with the Hans Christian Andersen Medal, which is named in honor of the Danish author of such classic fairy tales as "The Ugly Duckling," "The Little Mermaid," and "The Emperor's New Clothes." Based in Switzerland, the International Board on Books for Young People gives this award for lifetime achievement in literature in even-numbered years. O'Dell was the second American to win the award, and storybook author Meindert DeJong was the first. Although the Andersen Medal honors lifetime achievement, *Island of the Blue Dolphins* is the book on which O'Dell built his reputation as one of America's most important authors of historical fiction for young readers.

Scott O'Dell was born Odell Scott on May 23, 1898, in Los Angeles, California. The photo above was taken when he was about three years old, by which time his family had moved to San Pedro.

2

From Odell Scott to Scott O'Dell

SCOTT O'DELL WAS born Odell Gabriel Scott in Los Angeles, California, on May 23, 1898. He was the first child of Bennett and May Elizabeth Scott. A sister, Lucile, would follow eight years later.

The Scotts were distantly related to Sir Walter Scott, the nineteenth-century English novelist who would help establish the genre of historical fiction, but Bennett Scott's home was hardly the center of literary pursuits. O'Dell did not have fond memories of his father. Bennett Scott had little time for his children and was a strict disciplinarian. It was not surprising that in two of O'Dell's favorite childhood stories, Robert Louis Stevenson's *Treasure Island* and the nursery rhyme "Jack and the Beanstalk," the fathers were villainous characters.

O'Dell's mother was often ill. Elizabeth Hall, O'Dell's second wife, said that he spoke fondly of her, but more warmly about aunts and uncles. O'Dell grew up in a very old-fashioned family, where suppers were big events that could be attended by any number of relatives. As Hall explained:

> His family came from Ohio, both sides of the family. His mother and father were both from Columbus. They used to go back there every year to his grandmother's house and he used to describe the scene at the breakfast table. There would be all these aunts and uncles. His family was all do-gooders and Methodists, and they would spend their lives out there and most of the women didn't get married. They would be spinster-ladies. He would describe his grandmother at the head of the table, chomping away with her false teeth, and the toast which she would dip into her oatmeal. But he was a man who didn't have a lot of close connections and didn't talk a lot about his family.[4]

Outside the home, though, O'Dell led an active and adventurous life. The city of Los Angeles was far different from the way it is today. Although Los Angeles is now a major city with a population of nearly 4 million, when O'Dell was a boy, it was little more than a frontier town. Recalled O'Dell, "It had more horses than automobiles and more jackrabbits than people. The first sound I remember was a wildcat scratching on the roof of our house."[5]

O'Dell explored many hills, wooded areas, and acres of rocky scrubland when he was young. He and his friends

were constantly on the lookout to trap and catch small animals, such as lizards, snakes, and squirrels. One time, O'Dell
and the other boys caught an owl. It was an experience that
left a lasting impression on O'Dell, influencing both his fiction and his desire to respect nature, as he recalled:

> What did we do with this creature of the nocturnal air? We
> killed it, of course. We wrung its neck. We cut off its legs. For
> the exposed tendons of an owl's legs, when pulled in a certain
> way, made the tiny claws open and retract in a ghastly simula-
> tion of life. To this day, indeed to this very minute, I remember
> these depredations with horror.[6]

"THE BRIGHTEST BOY"

Bennett Scott worked as a stationmaster for the Union
Pacific Railroad, which meant that, whenever he was trans-
ferred to a new station, the family had to move. In fact, the
Scotts moved often during O'Dell's childhood, although the
family was able to remain mostly in southern California.
One of O'Dell's favorite homes was located on Rattlesnake
Island, now known as Terminal Island. It was across San
Pedro Bay from the coastal town of San Pedro. In fact, the
Scott home was right on the Rattlesnake Island beach, and
it was built on stilts so that it would remain above the ocean
when the tide came in. As a boy, O'Dell walked along the
beach, where he saw fishermen returning with their catches
of shellfish, such as abalone; then, he watched the fishermen
erect racks in the sun to dry the catch. Later, in *Island of the
Blue Dolphins,* O'Dell wrote how Karana caught abalone
and built racks to dry the fish in the sun. The time he spent
on San Pedro Bay undoubtedly provided O'Dell with a deep
appreciation of the sea. As an author, many of his books
involved adventures at sea.

The Scotts lived in many other places, such as the town of Claremont, which was east of Los Angeles near Mount Baldy. This rocky sagebrush country is where some of the first Spanish settlers made their homes in southern California, giving O'Dell insight into the local history. Living in this area gave O'Dell an opportunity to learn about Mexican culture, to develop an appreciation and knowledge of Mexican Indians, and to learn how they were abused and oppressed over the years.

By the time O'Dell was a teenager, the Scotts were living in Long Beach, a community just south of Los Angeles. He enrolled in Long Beach Polytechnic High School, where he earned good grades and competed on the track team. As a high-school student, O'Dell's favorite class was English, and that was when he first entertained the notion of becoming a writer. According to O'Dell, his teachers regarded him as "the brightest boy . . . they'd ever had or hoped to have."[7]

While O'Dell attended high school, World War I erupted in Europe. Soon after his graduation from Long Beach Polytechnic, O'Dell was drafted; he was inducted into the U.S. Army on October 9, 1918. The Army immediately sent him to Occidental College in Los Angeles to train as an officer, but the war ended just one month after his induction. O'Dell was discharged from the Army that December. He decided to remain at Occidental, where he planned to pursue his education and learn to be a writer. For O'Dell, the path to a college degree would turn out to be a bumpy ride.

"When I went to college I found to my great surprise that I was not the brightest young man in the world," he said. "Indeed, I found that most of my classmates were brighter than I was. Things had been so easy in elementary and high school, I hadn't needed to study. What's more, I didn't know how."[8]

LACKING FOCUS

O'Dell signed up only for courses that interested him: English, psychology, philosophy, and history. Although he knew he wanted to be a writer, his education lacked focus; he had no interest in the other courses that he needed to earn his degree, such as science and mathematics. Soon, O'Dell transferred from Occidental College to the University of Wisconsin. In the fall of 1920, he transferred to Stanford University in northern California. He remained at Stanford just long enough to join the boxing team and compete in a few matches, and then he dropped out after spring 1921. His time in college was not totally wasted, however, because his roommate in Wisconsin was Charles Rawlings, whom O'Dell introduced to a friend, Marjorie Kinnan. Rawlings and Kinnan would eventually marry. Both would become writers and both would carve out careers in literature: Charles Rawlings as a journalist and Marjorie Kinnan Rawlings as the author of the acclaimed novel for young readers, *The Yearling*.

After O'Dell dropped out of the University of Wisconsin, he returned to California, where he planned to pursue his ambition to become a writer. As a freelance journalist, he sold stories to several newspapers and magazines in the Los Angeles area. Until this point, he had been writing under his given name, Odell Scott. When a typographer at one of the newspapers mistakenly transposed his first and last names, spelling out his byline as "Scott O'Dell," he liked the way the name sounded and decided to stick with it. Later, he had his name legally changed to Scott O'Dell.

In 1919, O'Dell found a job with the Palmer Photoplay Company, which purchased photoplays for movies. Today, photoplays are known as screenplays, which are the scripts followed by actors and production workers. In 1919, no photoplays included spoken dialogue because a method of producing sound for film had not yet been developed. Therefore, all the photoplays obtained by the Palmer Photoplay Company were for silent movies. O'Dell's job was to read and critique the photoplays, and to find worthy scripts to produce as movies. O'Dell became something of an expert on photoplays: He taught a mail-order course to aspiring authors on how to write for the screen, and he wrote a book titled *Representative Photoplays Analyzed*.

VALENTINO, BARRYMORE, AND GARBO

By that time, Los Angeles was emerging as the capital of the American movie industry, especially the area of the city known as Hollywood. O'Dell found a job with the Paramount Motion Picture Studio, one of the biggest studios in town. He wrote photoplays and performed production jobs. He also worked with such movie stars as Gloria Swanson and Rudolph Valentino. In the classic movie *Son of the Sheik*, the script called for a close-up of Valentino holding a string of pearls. Since Valentino's hands were heavy and rough, the director feared they would not photograph well. O'Dell explained, "Valentino was a wonderful looking guy but he had butcher's hands, at least they came over that way."[9] He added, "Somebody happened to notice my hands. I was very slender then, young, and I had very aesthetic, long fingers. So they chose me to hold the pearls, and that was my only acting occasion."[10]

Therefore, whenever *Son of the Sheik* plays on nostalgia television networks or in classic film revivals at theaters, viewers who see that scene are generally not aware that the hands shown in the close-up do not belong to Rudolph Valentino, but to Scott O'Dell. "My only claim to fame!"[11] O'Dell once said.

O'Dell also worked for another large Hollywood studio, Metro-Goldwyn-Mayer (MGM), where he found a job as a cameraman. As an MGM cameraman, he traveled to Rome, Italy, where he filmed scenes for the original version of the movie *Ben Hur*, which tells the story of a Hebrew nobleman wrongly imprisoned by a Roman general. During this time, O'Dell helped make movie history: He used what is believed to have been the first color camera to make a commercial movie. Ironically, none of the film footage O'Dell shot in Italy made the final cut of the film. The director decided to return to Hollywood to film the entire movie in the studio.

While he was in Rome, O'Dell became friendly with John Barrymore, one of the world's greatest actors, as well as the novelist F. Scott Fitzgerald, who briefly made his home there. When his work on *Ben Hur* concluded, O'Dell decided to remain in Italy, where he took classes at the University of Rome. Later, he moved to the city of Florence, where he lived in a home once occupied by Galileo, the seventeenth-century Italian astronomer. In Florence, O'Dell wrote his first novel, *Pinfeathers*, which was intended for adult readers.

The novel was never published, and O'Dell left Italy and returned to the United States in 1927. He tried to write again, but met with little success. O'Dell lost money when he invested in the oil business and the stock market, and again when he tried to run a citrus farm. During this last venture, O'Dell wrote *Woman of Spain: A Story of Old California*, and this time, a publisher agreed to buy the novel. O'Dell also sold the book to MGM, which paid him $24,000 for

This photo of Scott O'Dell was taken in 1934, in the midst of the
Great Depression, when O'Dell was 36 years old. Because O'Dell had
sold the movie rights for his novel to MGM, he was able to live without
too much hardship at a time when most Americans were struggling to
make ends meet.

the movie rights and planned to feature the star Greta Garbo in the lead role. Although the movie was never made, the money O'Dell earned was an enormous sum in the late 1920s, and it enabled him to live comfortably during the Great Depression of the 1930s.

MODEST SUCCESS

On December 7, 1941, the Japanese attacked the U.S. Navy base at Pearl Harbor, Hawaii; the next day, America entered World War II. Some nine months later, at age 44, O'Dell enlisted in the U.S. Air Force. His second attempt to enter military service would prove to be as uneventful as his first.

At an Air Force base in Texas, O'Dell's job was to recommend service assignments for the inductees based on their intelligence. He gave each new inductee an intelligence quotient (IQ) test. A numerical score of 100 or above shows above-average intelligence. When O'Dell took the test himself and received a score of 140, the Air Force wanted to transfer him to New York City to a unit charged with deciphering enemy codes. O'Dell was not interested in this work, and he yearned for a role in the war that would provide him with some measure of excitement.

In 1943, O'Dell managed to receive a discharge from the Air Force, before he was shipped to New York, with the promise that he would find another way to serve his country during the war. He returned to California, where he joined the Coast Guard Auxiliary, the civilian arm of the service that protects the nation's shoreline. O'Dell volunteered to make night patrols in a small boat, cruising up and down the California coast in search of Japanese submarines. Hollywood star Humphrey Bogart, another member of the Coast Guard Auxiliary, often accompanied him on those missions.

A few months after the Japanese attacked Pearl Harbor, O'Dell enlisted in the U.S. Air Force. When he realized that his work with the Air Force would not grant him the excitement he craved, he secured a discharge from the Air Force with the promise that he would serve his country some other way.

The war ended in 1945, rather uneventfully for O'Dell. He began to write again and, in 1947, he published *Hill of the Hawk,* another novel aimed at an adult audience. A fictional account of the Mexican War, the book was his second attempt at historical fiction (*Woman of Spain* was the first), and it registered modest sales. Now in need of money, O'Dell sold his citrus farm and took a job as the book editor for a local newspaper, the *Los Angeles Daily News.* In 1948, he married his first wife, Jane Dorsa Rattenbury. They fought often during their 18-year marriage, which finally ended in a separation and then divorce in 1966. Later, O'Dell met and married Elizabeth Hall, a writer and magazine editor.

In the 1950s, O'Dell produced a large body of work, both fiction and nonfiction. While he was the *Daily News* book editor, O'Dell served as the collaborator on a nonfiction book titled *Man Alone.* Although he did not write the book, O'Dell polished the prose and edited the manuscript submitted by the author, a prison inmate who wrote under the name of William Doyle. *Man Alone* tells the story of Doyle's 20-year sentence on a murder charge.

After his contributions to *Man Alone*, O'Dell concentrated on his own work again, publishing the adventure novel *The Sea Is Red.* A work of historical fiction written for adult readers, it tells the story of the slave trade during the Civil War. His final book during this period of his life was *Country of the Sun*, a history and travel guide to southern California.

REACHING INTO HIS MEMORY

In 1960, at the age of 62, O'Dell had established his career as a modestly successful writer. None of his books was a bestseller, to be sure, but he earned a good living and was able to buy a comfortable home near the town of Julian, where he had spent some time as a boy.

It was while he lived in Julian that O'Dell found the inspiration to write the book that would define his place in American literature. In the late 1950s, O'Dell learned that hunters had invaded the Cuyamaca Mountains near Julian and were killing game in the region. It seemed to O'Dell that the hunters did not care what they killed; they were just interested in bagging game.

O'Dell believed he had to speak up for wildlife and the environment, and he thought he could reach more people with a book than by other activism, such as protesting. He decided to write a story in which a young person, who gives little thought to the plight of animals learns to live in concert with wild animals and appreciate the gifts they bring to the world. Reaching far back into his memory and recalling the story he had heard about the Lone Woman of San Nicolas, O'Dell decided to fashion a story based on the life of Juana Maria. He remembered:

> I heard about Karana, the heroine of *Island of the Blue Dolphins*, around 1920. I read a short article in *Harper's Magazine*, 1892. Just a brief, very brief, article about it, because little was known. It interested me at the time. I had no thought about doing a story about it; I thought it was interesting. And over the years it would crop up occasionally in writing about Santa Barbara or in newspapers you'd pick up. And then I got into a writer's block and I'd been writing adult books and I was in a place where I wasn't exactly satisfied with what I was doing. And I got this great hatred of the hunters that came into the mountains where I lived on the Mexican border, and that hatred combined itself with this memory of this

Did you know...

Did you know that two books by Scott O'Dell have been produced as movies? *Island of the Blue Dolphins* was released as a movie in 1964, and *The Black Pearl* was produced as a film in 1978.

The film version of *Island of the Blue Dolphins* was critically acclaimed. Actress Celia Kaye, who starred as Karana, won a Golden Globe Award as "New Star of the Year." Writing in the *New York Times*, film critic Howard Thompson said,

> Here is a gentle, frail and placid little picture about an orphaned young Indian girl, played by Celia Kaye, who finds a primitive home on a lovely, isolated island, learns the ways of the wild and its wild creatures. . . . The most attractive thing about the picture is the idyllic loveliness of the landscapes—rocky coastlines, gleaming beaches and azure skies. Scenically, at least, the film is perfectly in tune with the prize-winning novel by Scott O'Dell.*

In *The Black Pearl*, a young boy named Ramon finds a priceless black pearl in the sea near Baja, California. Ramon soon finds his life in danger from a rival pearl diver who is determined to own the pearl, as well as from a deadly manta ray that had been guarding the gem.

---

* Howard Thompson, "Island of the Blue Dolphins Has Premier," *New York Times* (July 4, 1964): p. 8.

legend about the girl on the island, 18 years old. One served as a catalyst to the other, and it became an idea: not for a book, exactly, but just something that I wanted to say, really to myself.[12]

O'Dell intended to write the book for an adult audience, but after he finished the story, he showed it to friend and writer Maud Hart Lovelace, the author of the Betsy-Tacy series of books for young readers. Lovelace told O'Dell that what he had written was a book for young readers, and she made some suggestions about how she thought O'Dell could improve the story. According to Elizabeth Hall, Lovelace told O'Dell that he had not made Karana feminine enough. Hall said, "She had absolutely no female traits. So that's when he put in the cormorant skirt. He put that in, and that softened her a little."[13]

O'Dell then gave the manuscript to his literary agent, who submitted the book to Viking Press, a major New York City publisher. Not only did Viking refuse to buy the book as it was written, the editors at Viking recommended a significant change: that O'Dell make the main character a boy. The editors believed that boys would never read the story if the hero was not a boy, and that girls only wanted to read about romance and were not interested in adventure stories. According to Hall:

> Viking said, "If you are serious about this book you'll change the girl to a boy," and Scott [told his agent], "Don't do anything, don't send it out again. I'm coming back East." So he got on a plane to New York, and they showed him the letter from Viking. He called his friends at Houghton Mifflin Publishers. They had published at least one or two of his books, and he had also written a chapter for them in another book. He had a very close friend there in the adult editorial department,

so his friend said, "I'll come down and we'll have lunch." And Scott said later that his friend kept thinking all the time during lunch, how am I going to tell my friend that I can't publish his book? But he took the manuscript home with him, and read it very shortly, and sent it to the head of Houghton Mifflin, and the president of Houghton Mifflin read the book, too, and he was wild about it. And so they called Scott, and said, "We want to publish your book." Houghton brought it out, and I think there was only one change made in it. The president wanted to know how she made those necklaces out of shells. So Scott stuck in a paragraph that told how she made the necklaces. And that satisfied him and everyone was happy.[14]

NEW PATHS IN LITERATURE

O'Dell had written for an adult audience for the last time. It had taken more than 60 years, but O'Dell's true talent as a writer had surfaced. *Island of the Blue Dolphins* would cut new paths in children's literature. Never had a book for young readers delivered such a strong message about the importance of living in concert with wildlife. Rarely had an author made a young woman into such a major character in an adventure story. As his career progressed, O'Dell would continue to write in the genre of historical fiction and use his books to call attention to many other important issues. O'Dell explained, "I have a sincere feeling that I am able to say something to children, that someone is listening. I am not just entertaining them; I hope somewhere in each of my books there is something they will take away from it that is important to them as a person."[15]

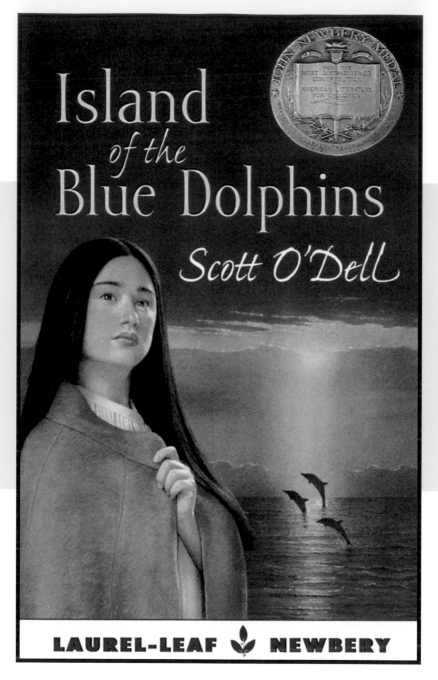

Above is one version of the cover for Island of the Blue Dolphins, *with the Newbery Medal emblem in the top right corner. The book was published in 1960, and it was awarded the Newbery Medal in 1961.*

3

Living in Concert with Nature

DURING THE 1960s, Americans woke up to the fact that they were doing serious harm to the environment. Rachel Carson's 1962 book, *The Silent Spring*, called attention to the dangers to wildlife, particularly birds, caused by the use of pesticides on farms. Later in the decade, Paul Ehrlich wrote *The Population Bomb*, in which he predicted that the overpopulation of the Earth would cause the environment to deteriorate. Meanwhile, few laws regulated emissions of pollution from cars and factory smokestacks, and few safeguards protected America's rivers and streams. Indeed, in 1969, a massive oil spill off the coast of southern California fouled the beaches and raised public awareness about pollution. By the end of the decade, Congress had passed the Clean Air Act and would follow up a few years later with the Clean Streams Act. Meanwhile, Earth Day, which is observed each year on April 22, was first set aside as a day for Americans to learn about the environment.

O'Dell's book *Island of the Blue Dolphins* helped children learn about the environmental movement in the United States. Published in 1960, the book raised many of the same issues that would be debated during the coming decade. As a novel that primarily reached an audience of children, it did not have the impact of the books written by Carson and Ehrlich; nevertheless, *Island of the Blue Dolphins* set the tone for the environmental activists who would soon argue that animals, fish, and birds have the same rights to the planet as people. Elizabeth Hall explained O'Dell's views, as follows:

> He felt that human beings had a responsibility to other species and that was one of the messages he hoped his readers would pick up from *Island of the Blue Dolphins*. . . . That was just part of him. He was always in nature, with nature [and] thinking about nature. He was concerned about the environment. He was concerned about oil drilling on the coast. And he was concerned about the depletion of fish, which was happening even then; not to the extremes that it is now, but people were beginning to be concerned and he was, too."[16]

Early in the book, before Karana is stranded, a ship arrives at the island. The Aleut hunters aboard the ship are hunting sea otters, which are prized for their pelts. Karana's father, the chief of the tribe, strikes a deal with the Aleut

A sea otter pokes its head above water. Sea otters are featured in Island of the Blue Dolphins; they populate the waters around the island until the Aleuts arrive and start killing them for their valuable coats.

captain: The hunters can kill as many sea otters as they desire, but they must pay the tribe for the pelts.

Sea otters are playful animals that are similar to seals, although they are smaller and their fur is thicker. When Karana sees the otters killed and skinned, she grows angry and worries that the hunters will wipe out all the otters on the island. Even though she has been promised a new necklace as her portion of the tribe's payment from the Aleut, Karana questions whether the jewels and trinkets offered to the tribe are worth the loss of the animals:

> Many of our tribe went to the cliff each night to count the number killed during the day. They counted the dead otter and thought of the beads and other things that each pelt meant. But I never went to the cove and whenever I saw the hunters with their long spears skimming over the water, I was angry, for these animals were my friends. It was fun to see them playing or sunning themselves among the kelp. It was more fun than the thought of beads to wear around my neck. (*Island of the Blue Dolphins*, p. 23)

POWERFUL FICTION

Soon, things go terribly wrong. The tribe and the hunters argue over payment, which leads to a fight. Many members of the tribe, as well as some of the hunters, die in the skirmish. Karana's father is one of the victims. The Aleut sail away with their otter pelts, and after a difficult winter on the island, the new chief decides the tribe must find a new home on the mainland. He takes a canoe east, returning several months later with a ship. The surviving tribe members board the vessel, but at the last minute Karana discovers that Ramo, her young brother, has left the ship to retrieve his spear. As the ship begins to sail, Karana dives overboard to remain on the island with her brother, because she knows he cannot survive alone.

Karana and Ramo settle into life on the island, but they soon discover that a pack of wild dogs is stalking them. The dogs kill Ramo, and Karana vows to kill the dogs in return, especially the large gray dog that is the leader of the pack. Karana fashions a spear and a bow and arrow, and she soon confronts the leader. When she shoots it with an arrow, the wounded animal runs away. Karana finds the dog a few days later, injured and dying, but instead of finishing off the dog, Karana takes the animal back to her camp to

Did you know...

In *Island of the Blue Dolphins*, Aleut hunters cheat Karana's village out of the payments they had promised for sea otter pelts. The hunters then kill many of the tribe members in a fight.

Scott O'Dell certainly portrays the Aleut hunters as the villains in the story, but the Aleut were themselves victims of harsh treatment. They are inhabitants of the string of islands known as the Aleutian Islands, which spread into the Pacific Ocean westward from Alaska. Expert sailors and hunters, the Aleut are related to the Eskimos.

In the 1700s, thousands died when Russians invaded the Aleutian Islands and forced the Aleut to harvest herds of sea lions, seals, whales, and fish. The Japanese attacked the far western islands of Attu and Kiska during World War II, taking the Aleut captive and sending them to prisoner-of-war camps in Japan. The Aleut also suffered when the U.S. government evacuated Aleut living on other islands in the chain; many died in camps in Alaska. Today, it is believed that fewer than 8,000 Aleut remain. Most live on mainland Alaska, rather than on the Aleutian Islands.

nurse it back to health. Karana names the dog Rontu, which means "fox eyes" in her tribe's language, and she and the dog become companions. Later, after Rontu dies, Karana befriends another wild dog, which she names Rontu-Aru, which means "son of Rontu."

Karana has changed through the course of the book. At first, she wants to kill the dogs and has no more respect for their lives than the Aleut hunters had for the sea otters. As she lived by herself on the island, close to nature, she grew to appreciate the life around her. When Karana found the wounded dog, she decided to save its life. In his book, *A Sense of Story*, which examined the works of several writers of juvenile fiction, children's author John Rowe Townsend said,

> *Island of the Blue Dolphins* shows a human being in changing relationship to animal life, about which the author knows a great deal. Birds, beasts and fishes are to Karana at first, and to a great extent must continue to be, either things to be hunted or competitors for the means of subsistence; but as she grows she achieves an acceptance of them as fellow-creatures. If there is a key incident in the whole book, it is the one in which she befriends her arch-enemy, the leader of the wild dogs.[17]

According to Hall, O'Dell had always harbored a love for nature. He preferred to live in the country rather than in the city:

> He didn't like to live in apartments and he appreciated nature. . . . He spent a lot of his time gardening. When we lived in Rancho Santa Fe, California, we had two acres there. And he spent most of his time, when he was not writing or doing research, out in the garden. And he had a deep appreciation for that. He loved the sea. The sea is everywhere in his books.

. . . And when we lived in Rancho Santa Fe we had a boat, a cruiser. And we used to spend a good deal of our time on it. We took it as far as Alaska. So the sea was very important to him, as were the creatures in the sea and the creatures on land. He always had a dog. At one time, before I met him, he raised cocker spaniels."[18]

Hazel Rochman, a writer and editor for *Book Links*, a publication for librarians, said that *Island of the Blue Dolphins* teaches important lessons to a group of readers who may not have been exposed to many stories about nature. The book is often assigned reading in the fifth or sixth grades. She said, "It's so powerful because it's fiction. It's all very well to have messages, but when you have a story that shows and tells, as this one does, it's very powerful."[19]

DEBT TO DEFOE

Island of the Blue Dolphins sends a strong message about preservation of the environment to its readers, but the book also includes a gripping adventure story. The book tells how Karana is able to endure the rigors and dangers of living alone on a deserted island for 18 years. Certainly, stories about survival have been popular among readers for centuries. Among the first is *The Life and Adventures of Robinson Crusoe*, written by Englishman Daniel Defoe in 1719, which tells the story of a shipwrecked sailor's survival on a remote island for 28 years. Later, readers would enjoy the 1812 novel *Swiss Family Robinson* by Johann Wyss. Modern movie and television fans have enjoyed the 2000 Tom Hanks film *Cast Away,* as well as the quirky cult television series "Lost," and the reality show "Survivor."

O'Dell has acknowledged his debt to Defoe and Wyss in *Island of the Blue Dolphins*. Although the two prior novels were mostly adventure stories in which people triumph over nature, *Island of the Blue Dolphins* takes the adventure a step further. The book shows how Karana at first fears the dangers of the island, then masters them, later comes to terms with the natural forces, and finally learns to live in concert with them. O'Dell explains, "In her brief lifetime, Karana made the change from [the] world, where everything lived only to be exploited, to a new and more meaningful world. She learned first that we each must be an island secure unto ourselves. Then, we must 'transgress our limits,' in reverence for all life."[20]

During her years on the island, Karana learns how to make weapons and build a shelter out of whalebones. She catches, dries, and cooks abalone (a type of shellfish) on her own. Although her tribe has left its canoes behind, the boats are damaged, so Karana learns how to patch the canoes and make them seaworthy. The canoes are also too heavy for her to carry, but Karana figures out a way to push the boats by laying a path with slippery kelp so that she can slide them down to the beach. Karana also fashions her skirt out of cormorant feathers. According to Townsend, "A Robinson Crusoe story has of course an appeal of its own which hardly needs to be spelled out. Survival is not an immediate problem at present for most of us in the civilized Western world, but as a theme it still touches our deepest inborn instincts and unconscious fears."[21]

LIVING WITHOUT LOVE

Even though Karana is able to build a shelter, make her own clothes, and find food on the island, she finds loneliness to be as much an enemy as the elements. As book critic Malcolm Usrey in the *Dictionary of Literary Biography* wrote,

> The book is more than one of survival; it is the story of great
> courage, endurance, perseverance, ingenuity, and, perhaps

most important of all, it is a story of a woman's surviving great loneliness and an even greater sense of isolation. It is Karana's loneliness and isolation that give the book one of its most powerful and universal themes, that all people need to be with others, to love and to be loved."[22]

Indeed, Karana learns that even though she has triumphed over the elements on the island, no one can live without love and companionship. For a time, she finds companionship in Rontu. Karana says,

> I would say, "It is a beautiful day. I have never seen the ocean so calm and the sky looks like a blue shell. How long do you think these days will last?"
>
> Rontu would look up at me just the same, though he understood none of the words, acting as if he did.
>
> Because of this I was not lonely. I did not know how lonely I had been until I had Rontu to talk to. (*Island of the Blue Dolphins*, p. 108)

Karana's story is truly sad. She loses both her father and brother, and she must endure years of solitude before she is finally rescued at the end. There is a feeling of optimism as Karana and Rontu-Aru stand at the rear of the rescue ship, watching the tiny island disappear on the horizon. Dolphins accompany the ship as it sails east, and Karana cannot help thinking of "all the happy days" (*Island of the Blue Dolphins*, p. 185) she knew on the island.

Island of the Blue Dolphins would prove to be an enormous influence on literature in America. Many other authors have touched on the themes raised by O'Dell in the book. In recent years, best-selling books that have delivered strong environmental messages have included such diverse novels as Cormac McCarthy's cowboy drama, *All the Pretty Horses*, Michael Crichton's science-fiction thriller, *Jurassic Park,* and Peter Benchley's gripping horror story, *Jaws*.

As for O'Dell, he would return again and again to the notion that humans must learn to live in concert with nature. In 1988, he published the novel *Black Star, Bright Dawn,* which tells the story of the Iditarod, the internationally famous Alaskan sled dog race from Anchorage to Nome. The central characters in the book are Bright Dawn, a young Eskimo girl who competes in the race, and Black Star, her lead dog. O'Dell based the character of Black Star on Nylack, his own Siberian husky.

During the course of the race, Bright Dawn is forced to seek shelter in an abandoned cabin, where she finds a mother wolf protecting her pups. At first, Bright Dawn is frightened. She worries that the wolf is a member of a vicious pack, and that the pack will follow the mother to the cabin. Instead, in a scene that recalls the relationship between Karana and Rontu, Bright Dawn bonds with the wolf and they decide to share the warmth of the cabin together. In the book, Bright Dawn says,

> Fighting sleep and bitter cold, I thought about what I should do. The wolf's eyes glowed yellow in the firelight. While she nursed her pups, she watched me.
>
> Overcome by sleep, I must have dozed, for when I saw her next she was sniffing at my hood. I lay still and spoke to her in the wolf talk I used with Black Star.
>
> She answered me in the same tones. The tones rose and fell. They were wild, not even close to being human, yet as clear to me as spoken words. She had accepted me. She trusted me not to harm her pups. (*Black Star, Bright Dawn* p. 80)

Sixteen years after publication of *Island of the Blue Dolphins*, O'Dell decided to continue Karana's story in the

In O'Dell's novel Black Star, Bright Dawn, *the Iditarod is the central event. Above, a competitor in the 2005 Iditarod drives his dog team along one leg of the race. The race was first run in 1973, and the course takes 8 to 15 days to complete.*

novel *Zia*. O'Dell's publisher, as well as his readers, had encouraged him to tell what had happened after Karana's rescue. In *Zia*, O'Dell picks up the story at the Santa Barbara Mission, where Karana meets Zia, her 14-year-old niece.

Of course, by now O'Dell was committed to the genre of historical fiction. He was well aware that Juana Maria, on whom the character of Karana was based, had died soon after she was rescued. O'Dell did not believe he could send

Karana on a new adventure, so he centered the story on Karana's niece and her young brother Mando, orphans who have lived at the mission since the death of their mother, Karana's sister Ulape.

Zia and Mando are aware that Karana has been left alone on the island, and they make a futile attempt to rescue her by sailing to San Nicolas in a small boat. After they return to Santa Barbara, Zia and Mando find themselves caught up in a rebellion that is being planned by the Indians who live and work at the mission. Indeed, much of the novel speaks to the plight of the oppressed Indians of the American Southwest, a theme O'Dell would visit many times in his career. Karana is eventually rescued and reunited with Zia and Mando. Although no one can communicate with Karana, when the family members first meet, Zia believes she sees a degree of recognition in her aunt's face. Zia says, "She must have known me at once because I looked like her sister. She touched my hand and held it for a moment. It was hard and rough and her nails were broken. I pressed my face against the bars and she did the same and our lips met there between them." (*Zia*, p. 134)

Karana dies soon after her rescue from the island. Although it is believed that Karana died of her exposure to germs, Zia does not think sickness caused her aunt's death. Instead, Zia believes life at the mission was too unfamiliar to Karana, and that her aunt died of homesickness for the island, the only home she had ever truly known. Meanwhile, Mando leaves the mission to join the rebellion. Finally, Zia realizes that she must also leave the white man's world at the mission and find her homeland. Accompanied by Rontu-Aru, Zia leaves Santa Barbara Mission and hikes into the mountains in search of her ancestral home. The message O'Dell communicates in this book is that Karana could not survive away from home. Fearing the same fate, Zia leaves the world of the white man to seek her homeland.

By the time *Zia* was published, O'Dell had become an important author of children's fiction. *Zia* was O'Dell's eleventh novel for young readers, most of which were written in the genre of historical fiction. It was a genre whose boundaries O'Dell would redefine as he told colorful stories of the American Southwest, the Crusades, the exploration of the American frontier, the Civil War, and many other exciting times in the history of civilization.

Above, Scott O'Dell relaxes on the deck of his boat, Perla Negra, *in 1972. O'Dell was quite prolific in the 1970s; he wrote 10 of his books in that decade.*

4

Telling History
Through Fiction

THE STORY OF Sacagawea is a well-known chapter in American history. The wife of Charbonneau, the guide on the expedition of Meriwether Lewis and William Clark, the Shoshone Indian girl soon emerged as an important member of the mission. She helped Lewis and Clark communicate with the Indians they met along the way, taught them how to survive in the wilderness, and served as a guide along the treacherous trail. At the conclusion of the expedition's 8,000-mile (12,800-kilometer) journey from St. Louis, Missouri, to the West Coast and back, Lewis wrote that Sacagawea "deserved a greater reward for her attention and services on that route than we had in our power to give her."[23]

There are many records of the journey. Lewis and Clark both kept extensive diaries during the expedition. Their diaries have been studied and interpreted by historians who have been able to piece together accurate accounts of what happened during the 29-month excursion. Indeed, historians have been able to confirm the importance of Sacagawea to the mission, a factor in the U.S. government's decision to place an image of Sacagawea and her infant son Meeko on the dollar coin in 1999.

Regardless of how carefully Lewis and Clark recorded the daily events of their mission, they did not write down the exact words the team members spoke to one another during the long months they were on the trail. Nor did they record details such as the ones O'Dell included: "It rained all night, hard. But in the morning, the land stretched away like a great silver lake. The far mountains glittered. The magpies flashed their black and white feathers. I picked a flower for Meeko to smell. Instead, he opened his rosebud mouth and tried to eat it." (*Streams to the River,* p. 90)

Scott O'Dell wrote that description of the North Dakota landscape for *Streams to the River, River to the Sea.* The 1986 book tells the story of the Lewis and Clark expedition from the viewpoint of Sacagawea, who is the main character in the book and the narrator of the story. Did the magpies flash their feathers? Did Sacagawea's baby try to eat a flower? Lewis and Clark certainly never recorded those details in their diaries. In O'Dell's book, Sacagawea's husband, Charbonneau, warns Lewis and Clark not to travel on the Missouri River by telling them the "Missouri winds like a snake." (*Streams to the River*, p. 91) Did he really say that?

It is likely that he did not. O'Dell made up the dialogue spoken by the characters, which is acceptable in the genre of historical fiction. Authors have been taking real-life stories and giving them a fictional twist for centuries. O'Dell's distant relative Sir Walter Scott is regarded as the first great historical novelist. His stories of adventure and intrigue in England and Scotland, including *Ivanhoe* and *Rob Roy*, are considered classics. Sir Walter Scott greatly influenced O'Dell; as a boy, O'Dell's parents gave him a complete set of Scott's works, and O'Dell read them cover to cover.

In America, nineteenth-century author James Fenimore Cooper's books about colonial times, including the classic *The Last of the Mohicans*, are considered to be as historically accurate as any nonfiction book written about the era. Another important example of historical fiction in America is *The Red Badge of Courage*, a novel about the Civil War, written in 1895, by Stephen Crane. Crane described what historians suggest is the Battle of Chancellorsville, although he never named the battle in the book. Crane did not fight in the Civil War, but his description is as detailed and precise as any eyewitness account.

A much more recent example of American historical fiction is *The Killer Angels*, written in 1974, by Michael Shaara. The book tells the story of the real officers and soldiers who fought in the Battle of Gettysburg during the Civil War, but Shaara made up the dialogue and placed his own words in the mouths of the characters, including Robert E. Lee, James Longstreet, and Joshua Lawrence Chamberlain.

SEEING HISTORY FOR HIMSELF

O'Dell uses the same techniques in several of his books, such as *The Road to Damietta* and *The Hawk That Dare Not Hunt by Day*. *The Road to Damietta*, which was published

Did you know...

Writers often compose stories in what is known as the first person, which means they tell the story from the point of view of the narrator. In the story, the character refers to himself or herself as "I."

Most of Scott O'Dell's books are written in the first person. O'Dell preferred to write in that style because he thought his readers would feel a greater connection to the events if they were able to assume the identity of the narrator, to be a participant. He said,

> I think writing in the first person is easier because you don't have to work so hard for suspension of disbelief. When you read that "I did it" there's a tendency to believe what you're being told. You get an almost automatic identification which I think is so important in a story.*

Other ways to write are in the second person and the third person. The author who writes in the second person tells the story from the point of view of the reader, but in the text the reader is referred to as "you." This approach is rarely used in fiction.

Much more common, though, are books written in the third person. Authors who write in the third person tell the story from the point of view of an outside observer. Characters in the book are referred to as "he" or "she," or by their names.

---

* Quoted in Justin Wintle and Emma Fisher, *The Pied Pipers: Interviews With the Influential Creators of Children's Literature.* New York: Paddington Press, 1975, p. 175.

in 1985, is a story about the Crusades into which O'Dell weaves a story about St. Francis of Assisi.

Born Francesco di Bernardone in 1181 or 1182, Francis cared for lepers and rebuilt ruined churches; later, he traveled with the Crusaders to the Egyptian city of Damietta to help lead the capture of the city. The Christians' victory was short-lived, and two years later, the Muslim armies drove them out of Egypt.

Francis is a major character in the book, but the central figure is Ricca Montanera, a 13-year-old girl. She falls in love with Francis and follows him, first around Italy and then to Damietta. Her love remains unfulfilled because Francis has dedicated himself to the poor and to the spread of Christianity. Still, Ricca pursues Francis all the way to Egypt, and she is with him as Damietta falls to the Crusaders, who set fire to the city and loot its treasures. Ricca says,

> Making our way through the swirling smoke, we came upon Francis. He was on his knees, his gaze upon the burning mosque. We spoke to him twice. He didn't look at us or answer. Suddenly he began striking his head against the stones. . . .
>
> The day after the Christian victory, Francis disappeared from camp. Brother Illuminato thought that he might be hiding in one of the mosques that was not ablaze. He was gone for more than a week, and when he returned he had little to say. He kept passing a hand over his haunted eyes as if to brush away a nightmare from which he had not fully awakened. And when Pelagius asked him to speak at a victory feast, seemingly in an effort to humble him further, Francis refused.
>
> "It is not a victory you celebrate," he told the cardinal. "It is a defeat and a humiliation." (*The Road to Damietta*, pp. 217–218)

In *The Hawk That Dare Not Hunt by Day*, which O'Dell wrote in 1975, the author once again uses a fictional character to tell the story of a real-life figure in history. The book recounts the story of William Tyndale, a sixteenth-century scholar who translated the Bible into early modern English. Although the main plot of the book concerns a young sailor named Tom Barton, the larger story describes the furor over Tyndale's translation. This eventually led to Tyndale's trial, and during the course of the book, Tom witnesses Tyndale's death.

Tyndale translated the Bible in the years prior to the era of European history known as the Enlightenment, a period when the leaders of the church and the state accepted new ideas. The Enlightenment is thought to have begun in the 1700s, but Tyndale lived in the 1500s, when new ideas were not so readily accepted. Scholars, scientists, teachers, and others who attempted to introduce new ideas and interpretations to society were often persecuted. Although Tyndale's words were at first regarded as a false retelling of the Holy Scriptures, his translation was eventually incorporated into the King James Version of the Bible. In fact, the King James description of Christ's Sermon on the Mount is essentially just as Tyndale wrote it. O'Dell believed that,

> Tyndale is important because he gave the shape, the thrust, the tone, and the elegance to the English language, which was pretty rough before . . . The King James version was put together a hundred years after Tyndale was burned at the stake for having translated the Bible. Two hundred forty-two words of the Sermon on the Mount are by Tyndale.[24]

Historical fiction can also be told without the use of real-life characters. In many books, O'Dell related historical events by using characters who were completely fictitious. *The King's Fifth*, which was published in 1966—it was O'Dell's first book following *Island of the Blue Dolphins*—tells the story of the Spanish conquistadors who plundered Mexico in the sixteenth century. The title refers to the law requiring the conquistadors to turn over a fifth of their booty to the king of Spain. The story is told through the eyes of made-up characters, among them a young mapmaker named Esteban, the evil captain Mendoza, and a priest, Father Francisco. Despite the lack of real-life characters, *The King's Fifth* is regarded as one of O'Dell's most historically accurate novels. In 1967, it was selected as a Newbery Honor Book, which is one of the most important awards for young people's literature.

To write *The Hawk That Dare Not Hunt by Day,* O'Dell decided to travel throughout Europe to see for himself the places where Tyndale lived and worked. Elizabeth Hall accompanied him on the trip. The couple traveled extensively through England, as well as through Germany, Holland, and Belgium, standing in the same places where Tyndale stood to recreate his impressions. As O'Dell described Tyndale,

> The man lived in attics and burrows and was pursued by spies all over Germany, Holland and Begium, attempting to seize him and take him back to England. His Bible was smuggled into England. It had to be, because it was against the law to own it or read it. He very calmly gave up his life for this purpose. He was a hero.[25]

IDEAS SURFACE AT ANY TIME

It was not unusual for O'Dell to do that type of research. According to Hall, O'Dell would often travel along the same paths as his characters. Indeed, he spent a considerable amount of time traveling along the route blazed by Lewis and Clark before sitting down to write *Streams to the River, River to the Sea.*

Scott O'Dell and his wife, Elizabeth Hall, traveled to Bayreuth, Germany, in 1970. There, O'Dell accepted the Federal Republic of Germany's Jugendbuchpreis *Award for his novel* The King's Fifth.

O'Dell said he found researching the story to be a much more enjoyable task than actually writing the manuscript. In fact, he said that to travel around the world, to follow in the footsteps of famous figures from history, and to read old books, newspapers, and other documents were the most fulfilling parts of the work.

"Writing is hard work," he said. "The only part of it I really enjoy is the research, which takes three or four months. The story itself as a rule takes about six months."[26]

According to Hall, O'Dell's ideas for books could surface at any time. For example, she said that O'Dell's 1989 book about the slave trade, *My Name Is Not Angelica*, grew out of a vacation the couple took to the Caribbean island of St. John, noting,

> Scott would pick a topic because it was something he wanted to know about. He was educating himself at the same time. Different books came about in different ways. I mean, *My Name Is Not Angelica* came about because we were vacationing on St. John and we were told the story about the slave rebellion and about the slaves who jumped off the cliffs. So Scott was not only fascinated by that, but we went back to St. John to do more research.[27]

The Hawk That Dare Not Hunt by Day had its beginnings quite differently. According to Hall, she was working at the time as the managing editor of the magazine *Psychology Today*. For a story for the magazine, she planned to interview George Steiner, a critic and professor at the University of Geneva. "So I was reading his books," she said,

> and Scott picked up one of his books of essays and started reading, and there was an article in it about the translator of the Bible, the hero, William Tyndale. So Scott was just abso-

lutely fascinated by the essay which told how much of the New Testament in the King James version was actually just lifted. So he said, "I want to learn more about this man. I think I'll write a book about him." So that's how that book came about. You never know what's going to spark a book.[28]

EARLY RISER

Once O'Dell conceived the idea for the book and finished his research, the time would come to write the story. As O'Dell said, it would often take him six months to complete the manuscript, although *The Road to Damietta* took about a year. *The Road to Damietta* is a work of historical fiction, to be sure, but O'Dell also intended the book to be a strong political statement against war. Indeed, *The Road to Damietta* was perhaps the strongest political statement O'Dell had made in one of his books since his call to preserve the environment in *Island of the Blue Dolphins*. "I'm going to take a full year for St. Francis," O'Dell told an interviewer while he worked on the book. "I want to get it right, it's an important book. In it, I'm going to make the strongest statement I can against war. It's simply dreadful the way the world is going. . . . This book will deal with the futility of war, the immorality of war, and I'm going to make it as strong as I possibly can."[29]

Since the 1920s, when he critiqued photoplays written by aspiring Hollywood screenwriters, O'Dell had always written on a typewriter; he once said that he enjoyed using an electric typewriter "because when you turn it on it has a little purr that invites you to start writing instead of looking out the window."[30] In his later years, O'Dell did much of his writing by writing out the pages of the manuscript in longhand. O'Dell switched to longhand after he quit smoking, because he found that whenever he sat at a typewriter, he needed a cigarette burning in a nearby ashtray. "I found that the typewriter was a part of this very bad and addictive habit, so much so that I couldn't go near it again," he said. "Now I write with a pen on a yellow pad."[31]

Actually putting the words down on paper could be a painstakingly slow process for O'Dell, which often commenced when he woke up at around 4:00 A.M. Before he got out of bed, O'Dell would go over in his mind what he intended to write that day. "Not line by line, but rather thoroughly," he said. "And when I get up, I walk the dog and I get breakfast and I'm usually at work by 5 to 5:30." [32] After he wrote for much of the morning, O'Dell would take a break, usually around noon. O'Dell had a unique way of ending his work for the morning. Rather than try to finish a chapter or even a page before quitting, O'Dell would often attempt to end his morning's work in the middle of a paragraph. "I know how it ends, so when I start writing I can pick it up at that point—and prime the pump, so to speak,"[33] he said. Then, after a few hours off to eat lunch, go for the mail, run errands, or do some gardening, O'Dell returned to his desk for another brief session at about 4:00 P.M. Usually, he worked for another hour or two, and then quit for the day. "But the story's never out of your mind,"[34] he said. Sometimes, he would spend much of his time rewriting. Many authors will not start to rewrite until they finish a chapter or perhaps the entire book, but O'Dell said he would often stop after a single paragraph and rewrite it several times. He admitted, though, that constantly rewriting very small parts of a book is probably not a very productive way to finish a manuscript. O'Dell suggested that young writers would do well to finish their first drafts before they go back to make changes, explaining, "If I were giving advice to a writer, I would say write very rapidly and go through your whole story rapidly and then go back and change things, because there is enthusiasm in that first draft."[35]

Scott O'Dell loved the sea and traveling, which he combined by taking his boat, Perla Negra, to places like Alaska, British Columbia, and Mexico. This photograph was taken on the boat in 1973.

5

Promoting the Rights of Women

SCOTT O'DELL WROTE nearly 30 novels, the great major-
ity of which feature girls or young women as main characters.
Beginning with Karana in *Island of the Blue Dolphins*, O'Dell
was one of the first American authors to realize that young
women had rarely served as the central characters in fiction,
particularly fiction written for young readers. Elizabeth Hall
noted that in O'Dell's books, "Even in the books that have
male characters as the lead there is usually a strong woman or
girl. Well, he felt very strongly that women could do just about
anything that men could do, anything they had the physical

strength to do, because he certainly felt there was no differ-
ence intellectually."[36]

Indeed, before O'Dell began to feature girls and young
women as his main characters, there were few books in
which a female had the leading role in the story, with the
exception of fairy tales. Hall remembered,

> The only strong females I knew when I was growing up and
> reading children's books were some of the women in fairy
> tales. You had the sister whose brothers have turned into
> swans and she manages to break the spell. So fairy tales
> occasionally allowed a strong female character. I used to
> read the *Oz* books, and the two main characters were women,
> Ozma and Dorothy. And Dorothy has to do things—figure out
> things—granted, but she always has her cohorts, the Scare-
> crow and the others to give her advice. It's not like Karana.
> Karana did it all on her own. I know Scott on occasion would
> get letters from boys, saying, "I don't know if a girl could
> do all that!" They don't write those kinds of letters anymore,
> although I sometimes get letters from boys saying, "I don't
> think I could've done that."[37]

Young readers could also find females as the central
characters in some detective stories. Beginning in the 1920s,
such teenage-girl sleuths as Nancy Drew, Judy Bolton,
Trixie Belden, Cherry Ames, and the Dana Girls were the
central characters in hundreds of detective stories that sold
copies by the millions. Nancy Drew is probably the most
well known character in the genre; she has remained popular over the decades, and many generations of girls continue
to read these stories. In 2004, a publisher announced plans
to revive Nancy Drew and feature her in a series of new
mysteries, and in June 2007, a movie called *Nancy Drew*
was released in the United States.

Was Nancy Drew a true role model for teenage girls? Nancy is certainly bright, attractive, talented, and independent. She drives a sports car, and her boyfriend is on the football team. Of course, at the end of each of her adventures she solves the mystery. In other words, Nancy Drew is the type of girl that every one of her fans would like to be. Nevertheless, whenever Nancy got into trouble, a male figure could always step in and handle the rough stuff, and it was typically her boyfriend, Ned Nickerson. Writing in the *New York Times*, critic Amy Benfer said, "She is an artifact of gentility, of primness, of an era when villains posed as members of the household staff to steal a family heirloom and girl detectives made sure their shoes and pocketbooks matched."[38]

Nancy was also expected to know her place, which was usually in a role secondary to men. In her book *The Girl Sleuth: On the Trail of Nancy Drew, Judy Bolton, and Cherry Ames*, author Bobbie Ann Mason discussed one Nancy Drew mystery, *The Haunted Bridge*, in which Nancy is called on to help a doctor administer first aid to an accident victim. The doctor is so impressed with Nancy's talents that he urges her to study nursing. According to the story, when she hears the doctor's words of encouragement, "Nancy flushed at the praise."[39] Why did the doctor urge Nancy to become a nurse rather than a doctor? At the time, Mason said, women were not expected to become doctors. "If girls cannot aspire to important careers in medicine and law and business, they can be rewarded for assisting men,"[40] Mason wrote.

WOMEN'S MOVEMENT

Island of the Blue Dolphins was published three years before another book that set the tone for the upcoming women's movement in America. Written by Betty Friedan, *The*

Feminine Mystique challenged the notion that women were not supposed to be strong individuals who were free to pursue higher education and professional careers. Throughout the 1950s, most American women were destined to serve in roles as wives and mothers who stayed home with the children. That changed in the 1960s, particularly after the publication of Friedan's book. In *The Feminine Mystique*, Friedan wrote,

> It was a strange stirring, a sense of dissatisfaction, a yearning that women suffered in the middle of the twentieth century in the United States. Each suburban wife struggled with it alone. As she made the beds, shopped for groceries, matched slip cover materials, ate peanut butter sandwiches with her children, chauffeured Cub Scouts and Brownies, lay beside her husband all night, she was afraid to ask herself the silent question—"Is this all?"[41]

Friedan may not have known it at the time, but she would have found a staunch supporter in O'Dell. "I have been appalled at the status of women," O'Dell told an interviewer. "Women have been treated as second-class citizens. I am . . . in favor of the women's movement. . . . I am trying to show that women and men do have the same potential."[42]

Indeed, O'Dell recognized that women were treated unfairly long before he wrote Karana's story. O'Dell said he first realized as a child that women were held back in American society. Growing up in turn-of-the-century California, O'Dell thought it was unfair that his mother did not have the right to vote. The Nineteenth Amendment to the U.S. Constitution, which granted women the right to vote, was not ratified until 1920. According to O'Dell, women have been pushed around and made really second-class citizens because their mothers were second-class citizens. In my lifetime, the women didn't have a vote. . . . The fight is not over yet. The argument being that they do have guts and that they can do things that men do, and that they need and deserve and have won respect.[43]

Hall believes that O'Dell was strongly influenced by his sister Lucile, and that it is very likely that Karana and many of the other females in O'Dell's books were drawn from the examples she set. According to Hall, Lucile was a strong-willed, active girl who believed she could compete with any boy. She was a bit of a tomboy, and she had a wild side:

I knew his sister; she was a strong gal. She was a rebel herself. She was eight years younger than he was and so he was an only child for eight years. And then his sister was born and she was sort of the *harum scarum* type, which got her into trouble, thumbing her nose at tradition and that sort of thing. . . . He talked about once, when she was 16, somebody came over with a motorcycle and she hopped on the back and roared off down the street. And since she was born in 1906, this was around the time of the First World War, and I don't know how many girls were riding motorcycles.[44]

THREE STRONG YOUNG WOMEN

Karana would, of course, become the first of many female protagonists in O'Dell's stories. Unlike Nancy Drew, O'Dell's heroines triumphed over their difficulties on their own, often battling not only nature but also the evilness of men. Three books by O'Dell that feature strong young women as central characters are *Sarah Bishop*, a story of Revolutionary War America; *The Serpent Never Sleeps*, a fictional account of the Jamestown colony in Virginia; and *Carlota*, a fictional account of the Battle of San Pasqual at the end of the Mexican War.

Written in 1980, *Sarah Bishop* is a historical novel, as is most of O'Dell's work. O'Dell and Hall had moved to the East Coast, buying a house in a rural portion of Westchester County, north of New York City. While he lived there, O'Dell had learned the story of a teenage girl who lost her family during the Revolutionary War and was forced to live in a nearby cave. The real-life Sarah Bishop met her troubles

Did you know...

Did you know that, throughout his career as an author, Scott O'Dell received as many as 2,000 letters a year from his fans? O'Dell said he was continually surprised at the questions posed to him by his young readers.

"In their letters, children ask dozens of questions," he recalled. "Some are personal, like 'How much money do you make?' but mostly they want to know how you work, how stories are put together, how long it takes to write a story, and what is the most important thing a writer should have."*

Occasionally, O'Dell also accepted phone calls from readers. In most of these cases, a class would call and the students would take turns asking him questions. One class truly surprised him, when the students wanted to know his favorite foods and hobbies. He answered,

My favorite food would be in the order of presentation: potatoes—fried, boiled, baked, head-on and dealt with them in her own way, and the fictional Sarah Bishop possessed the same degree of inner strength. In the book, when the evil Sam Goshen tries to assault her, Sarah fights him off, seizes a musket, and points it at her attacker: "I put it at full-cock. The sound came loud in the quiet dusk. His piebald horse was tethered nearby. I untied it and put my bundle across its back and mounted. I kept the musket pointed at Goshen all the time. 'I'll leave your horse at the tavern,' I said to him and rode away." (*Sarah Bishop*, p. 103)

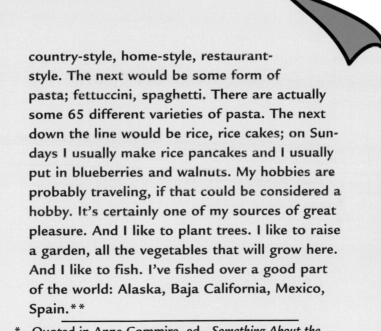

country-style, home-style, restaurant-style. The next would be some form of pasta; fettuccini, spaghetti. There are actually some 65 different varieties of pasta. The next down the line would be rice, rice cakes; on Sundays I usually make rice pancakes and I usually put in blueberries and walnuts. My hobbies are probably traveling, if that could be considered a hobby. It's certainly one of my sources of great pleasure. And I like to plant trees. I like to raise a garden, all the vegetables that will grow here. And I like to fish. I've fished over a good part of the world: Alaska, Baja California, Mexico, Spain.**

* Quoted in Anne Commire, ed., *Something About the Author*, vol. 60. Detroit, Mich.: Gale Research, 1990, p. 119.

** Quoted in *A Visit with Scott O'Dell*, Houghton Mifflin Author and Artist Series, VHS, 1983.

Published in 1987, *The Serpent Never Sleeps* tells the story of a young Jamestown colonist named Serena Lynn and her friendship with the Indian princess Pocahontas. According to legend, Pocahontas saved the life of the captured explorer Captain John Smith by pleading with her father, the Algonquin Indian chief Powhatan, to spare him. Many historians believe that this was not entirely true, since the captain was not above telling tall tales about himself to boost his reputation as a fearless explorer.

By the time Serena Lynn and her family arrive in Jamestown, the story of Smith's rescue by the Indian princess had circulated back in England. When they reach Virginia, the new settlers find that the colony has been devastated by starvation, and the survivors fear Indian attacks. Serena Lynn decides that to save the colony, she must find Pocahontas and convince the princess to spare the colonists. She wanders into the wilderness, locates the princess, and makes an appeal to her:

> The captain told me how you saved his life. . . . And more, you had saved the lives of many in Jamestown who were starving. I came to ask you to come to Jamestown again as you used to do. Then your father will look upon us more kindly. Then we will have more food to eat. Then we will not live every day fearful of being attacked. And you will not be fearful of us. (*The Serpent Never Sleeps*, pp. 140–141)

The two girls become friends, although it will take considerably more time before the Indians and colonists learn to live in peace. In fact, the colonists kidnap Pocahontas, prompting Powhatan to order an attack on Jamestown. The Algonquin agree to a treaty with the colonists only after Pocahontas falls in love with and marries John Rolfe, one of her captors. Still, Serena Lynn's courage in approaching

Pocahontas is vital to the ultimate fate of the colony. Later in the book, after she has married the colonist Tom Barlow, she displays her courage again. When Indians burn their cabin to the ground, Serena Lynn and her husband drive their enemies off, and then resolve together to rebuild their cabin, and their lives, in the New World. Clearly, O'Dell intended Serena Lynn to represent every woman in America the way he believed they should be represented: as strong and independent figures capable of showing courage and making their own decisions. "Through Serena's eyes we see the founding of America," (*The Serpent Never Sleeps*, p. 225) he wrote in the author's note at the conclusion of the book.

FORTITUDE TO BUILD A NATION

In 1977, O'Dell published *Carlota*, a fictional account of the Battle of San Pasqual at the end of the Mexican War in 1846. The central character of the story, Carlota de Zubarán, is perhaps one of O'Dell's strongest and most independent young female characters. Her father, Don Saturnino, regards Carlota as a replacement for the son he lost in an Indian raid, and Carlota fills the role with relish: She wears pants, races against men, and refuses to ride sidesaddle. Early in the book, while diving for gold coins hidden on a sunken ship, Carlota has a dangerous encounter with a giant clam that nearly bites off her hand:

> Putting my knees against the rough bulge of the shell, as the jaws opened and then began to close, I jerked with all my strength. I fell slowly backward upon the ship's deck. My hand was free. With what breath I had I moved toward the hole. I saw the sun shining above and climbed toward it. The

next thing I saw was my father's face and I was lying on the river's sandy bank. *(Carlota, pp. 35–36)*

The de Zubaráns are the owners of a California ranch. They favor neither the Mexicans nor the Americans in the war and simply want to be left alone. They are drawn into the closing days of the war when the American scout, Kit Carson, arrives at the ranch to warn them that a force of American soldiers is approaching; because the Zubaráns are Mexican, they are likely to be attacked. Don Saturnino summons the other Mexican ranchers, and they meet the Americans in battle in the San Pasqual Valley near present-day San Diego. The ranchers win the battle, but Carlota's father is killed.

Carlota is now the head of a 47,000-acre (19,000-hectare) ranch, which is an immense burden for a teenage girl. Following the battle, Carlota must guide the ranch through some difficult times when there is a deadly drought. O'Dell describes the devastation:

September passed and the drought grew worse. Every day a dozen more cattle died. The working horses we managed to feed by cutting branches from the willow groves along the stream. Our Indians caught rattlesnakes in the heavy brush, carried them across the barren mesa at dawn, and let them loose, telling them to beseech the rain gods. Doña Delores and I knelt at the altar and prayed. But the rains did not come. *(Carlota, p. 136)*

Facing foreclosure, Carlota returns to the river where she dives again for the hidden gold. Evading the giant clam, she retrieves the final few coins and uses them to pay off the debt on the ranch. The book ends on a note of optimism. Americans are moving into the valley, and Carlota realizes that she will have to find a way to live alongside the gringos if the ranch is to survive.

O'Dell describes Carlota's many ordeals: warfare, loss of her father, a drought, and two dangerous dives for sunken treasure. Carlota triumphs over the odds, just as Sarah Bishop and Serena Lynn had, proving that girls have the fortitude to survive and to help build a nation.

Scott O'Dell and Elizabeth Hall stand behind their grandchildren, Lauren and Scott Anderson. Lauren and Scott called O'Dell "Grampy." Here, he builds a tepee with the help of the "tribe" in 1980.

6

Stories
of Courage

SCOTT O'DELL SPENT much of his life in the American Southwest, and he was very familiar with the history and culture of the Native Americans of the region. They had suffered for centuries, first at the hands of the Spanish conquistadors, and then through the actions of the white settlers who pushed them off their land.

The plight of the Native Americans of the Southwest left a deep impression on O'Dell. He found himself sympathetic to their ordeal and has told their story in a number of his books. As his novel *Carlota* shows, O'Dell believed that Mexican Americans also endured years of abuse. His sympathy with the plight of abused people did not stop there. O'Dell wrote two books, *My Name Is Not Angelica* and *The 290*, which examined the slave trade in the United States. Elizabeth Hall explained O'Dell's sensitivity:

> He was especially interested in American Indians, because he felt for what had happened to them. When he went to college, he only took courses he enjoyed. He only took history, literature, and psychology. That's all he would ever take and he never got a degree. But he was a student of history, especially history of the Southwest and that was one thing that informed his books, because he was so aware of the way the American Indians had been treated by this country and by the army. And not only by the Americans, but the Spaniards, too—he was very concerned about that. He wrote one little book for younger children, *The Treasure of Topo-el-Bampo*, about the mines and how the Indians had to work under terrible conditions, and how they died like flies. And he was quite aware of that and he thought that kids ought to know about it. So he wrote many books on that.[45]

One of the darkest episodes in American history is known as the Long Walk, which was a 300-mile (480-kilometer) forced migration of some 9,000 members of the Navajo Indian tribe from their homeland in Arizona to a reservation in New Mexico in 1864. Although the Civil War was still raging, it was the era of manifest destiny, and Americans believed that it was their duty to spread their borders to the West Coast. In 1860, Congress passed the Pre-emption Bill, which provided free land to settlers in the western territories. The rush for land was on, and it soon became apparent to the Indians of the Southwest that white settlers, under the protection of the U.S. Army, would seize their fertile pastureland.

With the outbreak of the Civil War, however, the Indians felt they could resist the white settlers because the main force of the Army was diverted to fight the Confederates. In April 1860, the Navajo attacked Fort Defiance, a small Army outpost in Arizona. They failed to overrun the fort, but they inflicted many casualties. The Army responded by dispatching the scout Kit Carson, who now held the rank of colonel, into Navajo territory to kill Indians and take their livestock.

In January 1864, the Navajo made their last stand in Canyon de Chelly near Chinle, Arizona, in the far northeastern corner of the state. The battle was over quite quickly. The Navajo were cold, half-starved, and had few weapons. In fact, they could do little more than hurl rocks at Carson's men. Carson sent a message to the Navajo hiding in the rocks along the canyon walls: "You have until tomorrow morning. After that time my soldiers will hunt you down."[46] The next day, 60 cold and hungry Navajo warriors surrendered. A few months later, the Army marched the Navajo off their land.

O'Dell chronicled the story of the Long Walk of the Navajo in his 1970 novel, *Sing Down the Moon*. The main character is a courageous teenage girl, Bright Morning, a shepherd who rises up against her oppressors and declares that no army is going to tell her where to live. As O'Dell explains,

> Nowadays, people are dispersed, can live anywhere they want to. That's the trouble here in California—we're just a bunch of uprooted people. You don't know your neighbor and he never speaks to you. But this Navajo girl—she did want to go back to where her family had lived and have a child and live in a cave on the side of the Canyon. Even though she knows her people

were driven out, she still goes back and starts over again. I hope there's a lesson in this, an inspiration for children. It's very strong in me."[47]

Did you know...

Did you know that Scott O'Dell wrote two books for students in the elementary-school grades? *Journey to Jericho* was published in 1969, and *The Treasure of Topo-el-Bampo* was published in 1972. Although O'Dell usually writes in the first person, he wrote these books in the third person, which means that an anonymous outside voice told the stories.

In *Journey to Jericho*, 9-year-old David Moore and his family are on a trip across country to join his father in California. David travels by airplane, train, bus, and mule cart before he reaches his father's lumber camp. During the journey, David carries a jar of pickles that his grandmother has asked him to deliver to his father as a gift. David does his best to protect the jar, but in the final moments of the journey, when the boy is reunited with his father, he drops it. The jar shatters when it hits the ground, but by now preservation of the pickles seems a lot less important than it did at the beginning of the journey.

The Treasure of Topo-el-Bampo is set in eighteenth-century Mexico. It is the story of two burros, Tiger and Leandro, who are forced to work in a silver mine. The two burros escape from the mine with bars of silver strapped to their backs. After some adventures, they make their way to their former home in the village of Topo-el-Bampo, where the silver is used to help the poor people who live in the village.

FIRE OF THE HUMAN SPIRIT

The first half of the book chronicles Bright Morning's ordeal after her capture by Spaniards who sell her into slavery. She escapes and makes her way back to her Navajo village in Arizona. The American soldiers, whom the Indians call the Long Knives, arrive soon after Bright Morning's return and force the Navajo to leave their village. O'Dell describes the Long Walk through the eyes of Bright Morning:

> By this time there were thousands of Navajos on the march. We spread out along the trail for miles, each clan keeping to itself by command of the soldiers, who rode at the head of the column and at the rear. At night the Long Knives posted guards near all the Indian fires . . .
>
> For those who died, we scooped out shallow holes in the frozen earth and laid them there, putting rocks on the graves to keep the wild animals away.
>
> My grandmother was the second old woman to die. Somehow she got herself out of the wagon where she had been riding and stumbled off in the brush. She lay down and pulled a blanket over her head. She wanted to die and drove us away when we tried to help her. (*Sing Down the Moon*, pp. 97–98)

The Navajo are forced by the Long Knives to march to the Bosque Redondo Reservation near Fort Sumner on the Pecos River in New Mexico. By now, Bright Morning has married a Navajo youth, Tall Boy. The couple soon has a baby, but they face hardships on the reservation, and Bright Morning appeals to Tall Boy to return to their homeland in Arizona. Reluctantly, he agrees. They escape from the reservation and, after a difficult journey, arrive home and find shelter in a cave. The book ends on a note of optimism as Bright Morning and Tall Boy look forward to life on the Navajo homeland:

Rain had begun to fall. It made a hissing sound in the tall grass as we started toward the cave high up in the western cliff. Tall Boy had finished the steps and handholds and now stood under the cave's stone lip, waving at us.

    I waved back at him and hurried across the meadow. I raised my face to the falling rain. It was Navajo rain. (*Sing Down the Moon*, p. 134)

Despite Bright Morning's optimism, *Sing Down the Moon* is generally a dark story that illustrates the harsh treatment of one people by another. Still, O'Dell said he hopes his readers would come away with an important message, that even under the most difficult of times, the fire of the human desire to live free could continue to burn. He explained what motivated him to write the story:

In 1961 I spent part of the summer in Navajo country, where the states of Arizona and New Mexico, Colorado and Utah meet. This story about Bright Morning and her flock of sheep is the result of those days among the Navajos. I think of it as a modest tribute not only to this Indian girl but also to the courage of the human spirit.

    The fact that this spirit happened to be in an Indian girl is really incidental. I'm not interested in the Navajos particularly—they're not my favorite tribe, even. They were marauders—they rode in and took the crops of other Indians, after the harvest sometimes. But there was this thing that happened in Canyon de Chelly. Carson and the government rounded up the Indians and drove them to Fort Sumner. The important thing was the story. If the story is a good story children will read it for the suspense, and you can use suspense to do things. In *Sing Down the Moon* I wanted to call children's attention to the fact that there are such things as endurance, as loyalty to your family, loyalty to the place where you live.[48]

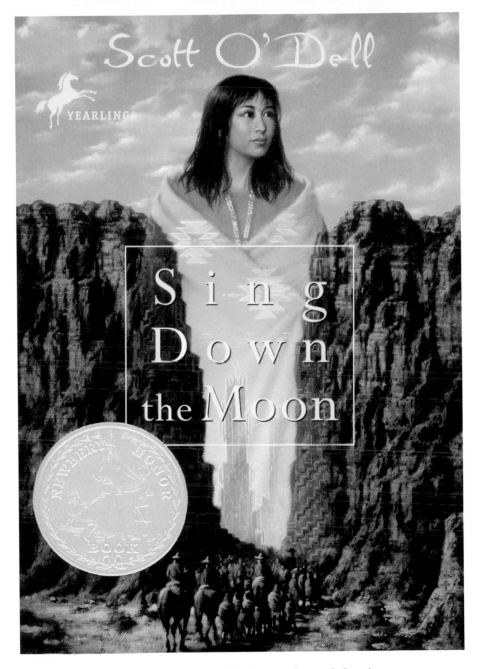

The plight of the Native Americans in the Southwest left quite an impression on O'Dell, who told their stories in several of his books, including Sing Down the Moon. This novel was published in 1970 and was a Newbery Honor book.

MANY VILLAINS

Between 1979 and 1983, O'Dell published three novels known as the Seven Serpents Trilogy. They include *The Captive* in 1979, *The Feathered Serpent* in 1981, and *The Amethyst Ring* in 1983. The books follow Julián Escobar, a young seminary student, as he accompanies the Spanish conquistadors and witnesses the abuse and conquests of the Mayan, Aztec, and Inca tribes of Central and South America.

To write the books, O'Dell did his typical research. Then more than 80 years old, he traveled as far south as the Peruvian Andes. Hiking high into the mountains to retrace the steps of the conquistadors, O'Dell said, "Your feet are lumps of lead and your breath comes in gasps, you live in these details as you write."[49]

Of course, the crimes committed against the Indians by the conquistadors are well known. In a search for gold and other riches, the Spaniards virtually wiped out the tribes, stole their land, and enslaved their people. In O'Dell's books, however, the Spaniards are not the only villains. Although the Spaniards are portrayed as evil and cruel conquerors, O'Dell also blames the religious leaders of the Indian tribes and holds them accountable for betraying their own people. In addition, O'Dell believes the Catholic priests did little to protect the Indians from oppression. In fact, Julián becomes caught up in the search for gold himself. In *The Amethyst Ring*, Julián joins the army of the conquistador Pizarro and watches as the Incan city of Macchu Picchu is destroyed by the Spaniards. Eventually, Julián realizes he has been corrupted by conquest and gold, and he returns to Spain, where he joins a monastery.

O'Dell also raised the issue of oppression in *The 290*, published in 1976, and *My Name Is Not Angelica*, published in 1989, but this time the victims are African slaves. Although

The Sacsayhuaman Fortress, near modern-day Cuzco, Peru, was an important military base for the Incas. O'Dell visited the fortress as part of the research for his 1983 novel, The Amethyst Ring. *O'Dell often traveled to the settings of his novels in order to enhance his descriptions.*

history has generally blamed American slavery on the white Southerners who relied on slaves to work in the cotton fields, O'Dell finds many other villains to blame in his books.

Indeed, *My Name Is Not Angelica* does not take place in the American South, but on St. Thomas, an island in the Caribbean Sea. The central character, Raisha, has been sold into slavery along with a boy, Konje, whom she had hoped to marry. The two African youths are packed aboard a slave ship with hundreds of others and forced to make a harrowing voyage across the Atlantic Ocean. Finally, they arrive at St. Thomas, where they are sold to a wealthy Danish family, the van Proks. In addition to her freedom, Raisha also loses her name. The van Proks rename her Angelica.

The slave owners emerge as villains, to be sure, but O'Dell also singles out the African chief who sold his people to the slave traders, as well as the *bomba*, the cruel black overseer who mistreats the slaves. As the brutality on the van Prok estate continues, the slaves start planning a rebellion. The book ends in tragedy when most of the slaves die by throwing themselves off a cliff after their rebellion fails.

FREEING THE SLAVES

The story of *The 290* may be more familiar to American readers. The title refers to a Confederate warship built in Liverpool, England. Great Britain was officially neutral during the war, even though British leaders openly backed the South. The warship was referred to by number to maintain secrecy, but it was eventually christened the *Alabama* and went on to sink 69 Union ships over the course of the Civil War.

O'Dell did not intend *The 290* to be simply about adventure on the high seas. The story centers on Jim Lynne, a

16-year-old sailor in the Confederate Navy, who stays loyal to the cause, even though he harbors deep doubts about slavery. Jim has run away to escape the stern discipline of his father, who is a New Orleans slave trader. Aboard ship, Jim helps suppress a mutiny, which gains him the favor of the captain. Later, as the 290 sails through the Caribbean, Jim is sent on a mission to Haiti, where he discovers that his father is running a slave camp. Although the navy is devoted to maintaining slavery as a way of life, Jim resolves to free the slaves from his father's camp. Jim feels ambivalent: He has no love for slavery but, as a southerner, he feels a duty to support the Confederacy. He also feels hostility toward his father because of his past treatment and has no qualms about destroying his business.

After Jim leads 100 slaves to freedom, he provides them with tools and takes them to a remote island in the Caribbean, where they hope to carve out new lives. Jim says,

> The island seems to be solid jungle made up of several different kinds of trees, many of them bearing fruit. Where these trees grew, so would berries, edible roots, and yams. The people had tools to fell the forest and till the soil. They had a plentiful supply of running water. The supplies from the ship would tide them over until they could grow a crop of melons, whose dried husks I saw along the shore and the edge of the jungle. (*The 290*, p. 85)

My Name Is Not Angelica, The 290, Sing Down the Moon, and the books of the Seven Serpents Trilogy show that O'Dell could be passionate about the wrongs committed against blacks, native Americans, and others. O'Dell felt a duty to speak up for all oppressed people, just as he felt a duty to speak up for women's rights and the environment.

Kelsey Bay is a small settlement on Vancouver Island in British Columbia, Canada. Scott O'Dell visited the area and posed for this photograph in 1970.

Troubled Teenagers

CHILD OF FIRE, written in 1974, represents a significant departure in O'Dell's style as a storyteller. The narrator is an adult rather than a young person: California juvenile parole officer Ben Delaney, whose job calls for him to track down young delinquents and help them straighten out their lives. Although O'Dell weaves episodes from the past into the story, the book does not belong in the genre of historical fiction. He discusses the story of Coronado, the Spanish explorer who discovered the Grand Canyon, the Painted Desert, and then made his way as far as Kansas. Despite this, *Child of Fire* is a contemporary story that addresses gang violence, drug use, and other issues faced by young people in today's society.

The book opens at a bullfight, which is a sport that angers animal rights activists because of its cruelty to the bulls. Although it is outlawed in the United States, bullfighting is legal and very popular in Mexico, Spain, and a handful of other countries. Delaney explains early in the book that he is not a fan of the bullfights, but he often accompanies Lieutenant Morales, a Mexican policeman, to the bullring whenever he has to go to Tijuana, Mexico, to confer with Morales on a case. Tijuana is just across the border from San Diego County.

The story is really about Manuel Castillo, a 16-year-old dropout and gang leader whom Delaney and Morales encounter at the bullfight. O'Dell writes,

> I was aware that the boy would be locked up unless he could buy his way off, which didn't seem likely. There was a good chance he would be sent to San Tomás prison for a couple of months. But I really didn't mean to get myself into it. I already had a heavy work load—forty-two boys that I was responsible for. All I could take care of. I was really surprised when I heard myself say, "Manuel here lives in Mar Vista. It's my territory. I'll take him home and keep an eye on him." (*Child of Fire*, p. 30)

Manuel is intelligent, good-hearted, and a natural leader, traits that Delaney does not see in many of the juvenile delinquents he supervises. He convinces Manuel to return to school, but Manuel soon has trouble fitting in. Unable to break free from his past, Manuel gets involved in a shootout with a rival gang leader. During the shootout, which occurs during a drug deal, Manuel kills a gang member, but his shot saves Delaney's life.

Manuel's life takes a new turn when he leaves the gang life to become a union organizer. A local grape farmer who employs Hispanic workers has decided to automate his vineyard, which will put many of the Hispanic pickers out of work. O'Dell modeled Manuel's story on the life of Cesar Chavez, the Mexican-American union organizer from California who led a number of farm-labor uprisings during the 1960s and 1970s. Chavez led many campaigns against the wealthy California grape growers, whose crops are vital to the manufacture of wine. After many years, Chavez was able to win higher wages and health benefits for the grape pickers.

LABOR ORGANIZER

At this point, O'Dell does borrow from history to help move the story along. Although Chavez preached nonviolence, the farm owners often hired thugs to keep union organizers away from the workers. Occasionally, the union organizers would resort to violence themselves. In 1973, just a year before *Child of Fire* was published, one California farm-labor leader was killed in a confrontation with police, and another was murdered by thugs hired by the growers.

A similar situation surfaces in the labor dispute at the center of *Child of Fire*. Emotions start boiling as Manuel, now called Manny, learns that the growers plan to start using the automated grape picker on a local farm. In the book, Manuel tells Delaney that he is thinking of blowing up the automated picker:

> "Three Chavez men came to our camp last night," Manny said. "They brought some food and told us not to fight. If we

don't fight they will help us. But three other men came last night and wanted us to fight. They had bombs, Coke bottles with wicks and gasoline in them. 'A truck load of bombs,' they said, 'enough bombs to burn up the vineyard!' 'The vines are green,' I said, 'and they won't burn.' 'The grass around the vines will burn,' they said, 'and the smoke will ruin the grapes.'" (*Child of Fire*, p. 205)

Manuel ultimately decides not to use violence, but the labor demonstration against the automated picker ends in tragedy. This is another O'Dell book that concludes with a truly sad ending, but there is no question that he addresses many contemporary social issues. The justice sought by the farm laborers is certainly central to the story, but the book also attempts to show young people the futility of a life of gang violence and drugs.

Although *Child of Fire* was not a historical novel, O'Dell once again thoroughly researched the subject before he sat down in front of his typewriter. To learn about delinquent youths and the job of the parole officer, Elizabeth Hall said that O'Dell rode with a San Diego parole officer as he visited the youths he supervised. O'Dell also visited a halfway house, which is a residential facility where troubled youths live while they are either working in the community or going to school. Once they prove that they can function as law-abiding, responsible members of the community, the halfway-house clients are permitted to return home.

According to Hall,

When he was researching *Child of Fire*, he sought out a parole officer in San Diego and he went around with him, and there was a halfway house and he became a board member of the halfway house and he met the boys that were living there.

Did you know...

Scott O'Dell was a fan of many writers who helped shape his own writing style. Among the authors O'Dell enjoyed reading were Joseph Conrad, author of a dark story about a voyage through Africa titled *Heart of Darkness*; F. Scott Fitzgerald, author of the classic American story *The Great Gatsby*; Willa Cather, who wrote books about the struggle to survive on the American frontier such as *My Ántonia*; and Herman Melville, author of the classic novel about whale hunters, *Moby-Dick*.

O'Dell particularly liked Melville's work. In fact, his 1968 novel, *The Dark Canoe*, includes many references to Moby-Dick and could even be considered a sequel to Melville's 1851 novel. O'Dell's book tells the story of the *Alert*, a ship in search of a wrecked whaling vessel, the *Amy Foster*. The character of Caleb is based on Ahab, the captain of the doomed whaler *Pequod* in *Moby-Dick*. In one scene in the book, Caleb nails two gold coins to the mast of the ship and offers them as a reward to the crew member who first sights the *Amy Foster*. Ahab offered a similar reward to his men in his search for the monster whale, Moby-Dick.

During the story, the crew of the *Alert* finds a coffin they believe was fashioned by Queequeg, the Indian harpooner who sailed on the *Pequod*. The discovery prompts the men to consider a search for Moby-Dick themselves. In the end, they decide they would suffer the same fate as Ahab and his crew, and instead the *Alert* returns to its home port in Massachusetts.

And he talked to them to get a feel for his characters in *Child of Fire*.[50]

O'Dell did stick to one familiar theme in *Child of Fire*. His portrayal of the bullfight definitely reminds his readers how much he abhorred cruelty to animals. Later in the book, the characters participate in a cockfight, which is an illegal sport in which participants gamble on roosters that fight one another in a pit. Typically, spurs are clamped onto the roosters' feet, which they use to slash at each other. O'Dell describes the cockfight as a truly vicious spectacle:

> Both gamecocks were dying. But who would be the first to die? The crowd was quiet. The boys were on their knees at opposite sides of the pit. The referee looked at his watch and waited. There were still a few minutes to go before the time limit was up. (*Child of Fire*, p. 128)

Child of Fire included vivid descriptions of the gang life, drug warfare, and other social ills of the Hispanic community on both sides of the border. After publication, members of the Hispanic community criticized O'Dell for his harsh portrayal of their life. O'Dell, who had spent many years in the Southwest, often quite near the border with Mexico, felt he was able to tell Manuel's story, but the New York Council for Interracial Relations disagreed.

The civil rights group suggested that since O'Dell was not Hispanic, he was not qualified to write such a book. O'Dell reacted strongly to the group's criticism, arguing that it was foolish to think this way. After all, he noted, nonblacks had written stories about the plight of blacks in America, and male authors had written stories about women.

He argued further,

This group started out originally on a soap box, saying that a white man or a white woman should not write about blacks, that only blacks could write about blacks, which is arrogant nonsense. That automatically rules out practically all of literature. For example, there's *Anna Karenina*, the greatest story ever written about a woman, and it was written by Tolstoy, a man. Well, this group got off this very quickly because they were in quicksand, and they realized it. . . .This is a very dangerous group. To paraphrase Thomas Jefferson, tyranny always begins in an excess of virtue.[51]

LSD TRIP

Four years later, *Kathleen, Please Come Home,* another book about a troubled teenager, was published. This time, O'Dell did not pepper the story with such subplots as the history of the farm-labor movement or an explanation of Coronado's expedition to America. Instead, *Kathleen, Please Come Home* is told in the form of diaries kept by 15-year-old Kathleen and her mother. These diaries soon reveal that Kathleen is a drug abuser and pregnant runaway.

O'Dell even has Kathleen write about her experiences under the influence of the hallucinogenic drug lysergic acid diethylamide (LSD), which was something of a literary challenge for the writer. At the time of publication of *Kathleen, Please Come Home*, O'Dell was 80 years old and hardly in a position to know firsthand what it was like for a teenager to be tripping on LSD. Still, he did manage to walk Kathleen through the experience:

As I spoke the poem, the words glided out of my throat and hung in the air. They no longer were little squares but hovering butterflies that looked like jewels. Oh, so sweet and beautiful. . . . Music came from far off. It was the music of stars rubbing together, touching, lingering, kissing—millions of stars, and I was a star, too. . . .

    I was richer than anyone in the world, than anyone who ever lived. . . . Then an angel's hand plucked me from the tree and I floated earthward like a dandelion puff in a soft, soft breeze full of friendly voices and the odors of all the perfumes in the world.[52]

During the course of the book, Kathleen suffers many losses. She loses her best friend to a drug overdose; she loses her baby in an automobile accident; and, finally, she loses her mother, who has sold her house so that she may travel the country in search of Kathleen. O'Dell tackled some very tough issues in the book, but critics agreed that O'Dell was able to tell a fulfilling story. Writing in the *World of Children's Books*, critic Sally Rambaugh said, "*Kathleen, Please Come Home* is the story of change, an honest rendition of the struggle and hardships involved in the growth from innocence to maturity. On this level, the novel is . . . deeply moving and profound."[53]

COCAINE AND SPONGES

Another O'Dell book that examines contemporary issues is *Alexandra*, published in 1984. Unlike *Child of Fire* and *Kathleen, Please Come Home*, his previous two books, *Alexandra* starts out as an adventure story. The main character, Alexandra, is a member of a family of Greek sponge divers who dive in the string of islands known as the Florida Keys. To research *Alexandra*, O'Dell spent time in the Keys, and he discovered many newspaper stories written about sponge diving in the 1920s by Charles Rawlings, his former college roommate in Wisconsin. The Rawlings articles proved to be invaluable to O'Dell as he prepared to write the book.

Above, Scott O'Dell poses for a photograph in Florida in 1983. O'Dell visited Florida to do research for his novel set in contemporary times, Alexandra.

Most sponges bought in grocery stores are made of artificial substances that absorb water and cleaning fluids. In his research, O'Dell learned that there are natural sponges, which are animals whose skeletons have a great capacity to absorb fluids. The sponges live along the ocean floor and are retrieved by divers, who usually have to wear breathing equipment while they harvest the animals. Once on dry land, the skeletons dry out, and can then be cut into squares and sold as a cleaning tool. Natural sponges are usually far more expensive than artificial ones, but they are also far more effective cleaners.

When Alexandra's father dies in a diving accident, Alexandra replaces him on her grandfather's boat and soon becomes one of the best divers in the Keys. In a scene reminiscent of Carlota's battle with the giant clam, Alexandra confronts a fierce saltwater turtle, and she becomes something of a local celebrity. Alexandra soon falls in love with a young shrimp fisherman, Spyros Stavaronas, but Spyros is more interested in Daphne, Alexandra's older sister.

Meanwhile, Alexandra becomes suspicious of Steve Parsons and Tasso, a pair of deckhands on the boat who both carry large wads of cash. Soon, she comes across a supply of the drug cocaine stashed amid the sponges. Alexandra says,

> As I stamped water from the last of the sponges, I saw what looked to be a cigar wrapped in plastic film lying on the deck. I took it to be one that Steve Parsons had dropped by mistake.
>
> I picked it up and was about to lay it aside to give to him when the plastic wrapping cracked and I saw that instead of tobacco it contained a white powder like sugar. Instantly, I thought of a movie I had seen at school about the dangers of cocaine. The powder in the movie and the powder I held in my hand looked exactly alike. (*Alexandra,* p. 94)

Alexandra eventually concludes that her sister's boy-friend, Spyros, is involved in the cocaine ring. By now, Spyros and Daphne have announced their plans to marry. Alexandra wrestles with her conscience: If she reports the cocaine to the authorities, it would surely mean that Spyros would be arrested. When Alexandra finds a vial of cocaine in her sister's purse, she makes up her mind and notifies the police.

Certainly, *Alexandra* does not include the harsh social lessons readers could find in *Child of Fire* and *Kathleen, Please Come Home*. Nevertheless, Alexandra realized when she found the vial of cocaine in her sister's purse that drug abuse had now invaded her family. She chose the only course of action available to her.

Scott O'Dell talks with children at an Indianapolis school in April 1981. O'Dell was in Indianapolis to deliver the Marian McFadden Lecture at the Indianapolis Public Library. Each year, the library invites a renowned author to deliver the lecture; other speakers have included John Irving, Louis Sachar, and Judy Blume.

Following in O'Dell's Footsteps

THUNDER ROLLING IN the Mountains is O'Dell's twenty-seventh book for young readers. It tells the story of the tragic plight of the Nez Perce Indians, who were driven off their land in Oregon and Idaho, then forced to flee to Canada. The narrator, the Indian girl Sound of Running Feet, is the daughter of the chief of the Nez Perce.

Early in the book, Sound of Running Feet sees white men panning for gold in a creek that feeds the Wallowa River near her home. When she tells her father what she has witnessed, the chief recognizes it as a dim omen of the future. "We are few and they are many," the chief says. "They will devour us."[54]

The Indians and whites skirmish, and eventually the soldiers arrive to drive the tribe off its land. The Nez Perce win one battle, but they are betrayed by another tribe and captured. Sound of Running Feet escapes and searches for Sitting Bull, the great Sioux Indian leader, hoping to convince him to intervene. Although she finds the chief, she cannot persuade him to come to the protection of the Nez Perce. Most of the tribe is forced to remain in Canada, far from their homeland. Sound of Running Feet's father dies in the Washington territory, a broken man.

O'Dell has returned to some familiar themes. *Thunder Rolling in the Mountains* uses the genre of historical fiction to tell of the plight of an oppressed people, as well as to make a strong statement against war. Through the voice of the Nez Perce chief, O'Dell declares: "All men are made by the same Great Spirit Chief. Yet we shoot one another down like animals."[55]

O'Dell never finished the book. He died on October 15, 1989, at age 91. Elizabeth Hall completed *Thunder Rolling in the Mountains,* and it was published in 1991.

THE SCOTT O'DELL AWARD

Before O'Dell died, he took steps to ensure that historical fiction would continue to be an important part of children's literature. In 1982, he established the Scott O'Dell Award for Historical Fiction. Since then, more than 20 writers have won the award, which includes a cash prize of $5,000. A committee of editors and librarians selects the winners.

Although it is sometimes difficult for the committee to choose from the many talented authors, in some years, no one wins the award. Hazel Rochman, a *Book Links* editor who serves on the selection committee, said the panel has decided from time to time that no book has met the high standards for historical fiction set by O'Dell in his own work. In recent years, though, that has not been a problem. She said,

> At least at first, there were just a few great titles to consider. But now, things couldn't be more different—and more difficult. The last few years we have had shelves of exciting historical fiction, and many of the books are so good that it's been very hard to choose just one winner. [56]

According to Rochman, there are many writers today who make significant contributions to the genre of historical fiction. Richard Peck, one writer who follows in O'Dell's footsteps, won the O'Dell Award in 2004 for *The River Between Us*. Rochman explained that, "He was absolutely moved that he got the Scott O'Dell Award because Scott O'Dell was his hero."[57]

The River Between Us is set during the time between the Civil War and World War I. It tells a story of families who are racially mixed during an era when it was not socially acceptable for blacks and whites to marry or have children together. Like O'Dell, Peck did extensive research before sitting down to write *The River Between Us,* and he did a lot of his research in libraries. He said,

> I go to the library with a partially open mind because I know that in the open stacks of a real old-fashioned library, the sort I go to, there's going to be a book there that's going to lead me in a new direction. It's going to give me a piece of information. Like the fact that you drop an egg into the radiator of a Ford Model T so that it will hard-boil and seal the leaks. That's the most praised line in *The River Between Us*. I learned it in the library. In 1916 they would have been driving a car and what kind of car would it have been? It would have been a Ford.

And what kind of roads? Those were roads where you had to turn around and go up in reverse. So I read car manuals of 1916. I was trained to do research.[58]

TEACHING HISTORY

Peck insists that historical novels could be used to teach history. Although English teachers often assign the works of O'Dell and other novelists to their students, Peck believes that the research performed on some novels is so thorough that history teachers could make use of them as well. He said that is particularly true during times of war.

Peck added that many students do not understand wars and why they are fought. Certainly, young people can find answers to many of their questions about wars and conflict in the newspapers or during television newscasts, but students may have little interest in following the headlines on a regular basis. On the other hand, Peck thinks that a historical novel about war may help them understand why modern wars are fought. Often, young people harbor an "illusion that they're immune" from the truth about modern warfare, but Peck believes, "A story set in the past can ask a modern reader timeless questions about all those issues history and progress never solve."[59]

Hazel Rochman also believes historical fiction could be a valuable tool for history teachers. A well-researched novel can catch and hold a reader's attention, and it can probably teach as much about history as a nonfiction textbook. She said, "I think one of the things that's so important is that these writers love the research and they love the history. And they do the research. Then, as a fiction writer, they can actually tell the story without letting all that documentary detail overwhelm the story."[60] According to Rochman, weak writers do the research, and then they want to impress the readers with how much they know about the subject. "They'll lean over backwards to show you that they've done their research and then it's so boring. . . .They're so busy proving to themselves," [61] she explained. O'Dell avoided making his characters perfect, which is a pitfall that other authors fall into, particularly authors who write about minority groups or other unfamiliar people. Since the writer is not a member of that race or religion, he or she may try very hard not to offend members of that group. All of the main characters in O'Dell's books had their weaknesses, and they made their mistakes. In fact, O'Dell's critical treatment of some Hispanics in *Child of Fire* did lead the New York Council for Interracial Relations to level some criticism at him. Said Rochman, "Making [them] perfect is the most demeaning and boring thing, which I think is a problem. Somebody could be heroic but not perfect."[62]

STRONG WRITERS

Other O'Dell Award winners whom Rochman admires are Avi, the 1985 winner for *The Fighting Ground*; Patricia MacLachlan, the 1986 winner for *Sarah, Plain and Tall*; Karen Hesse, who was selected for the award in 1998 for her book, *Out of the Dust*; Mary Downing Hahn, who won the O'Dell Award in 1992 for *Stepping on the Cracks*; and Mildred D. Taylor, who received the award in 2002 for *The Land*.

Rochman thinks these writers follow in O'Dell's footsteps because, like O'Dell, their historical fiction is not centered on notable figures in history. Famous figures do turn up in O'Dell's fiction: St. Francis of Assisi in *The Road to Damietta*; Kit Carson in *Sing Down the Moon;* and Pocahontas in *The Serpent Never Sleeps*. O'Dell focused instead on

Did you know...

Scott O'Dell wrote 27 books for young readers. All but one of his books were novels.

His single nonfiction book for young readers was *The Cruise of the Arctic Star*, which chronicles a voyage O'Dell made with his wife, Elizabeth Hall, along the Pacific Coast in the *Arctic Star*, their 50-foot (15.25-meter) boat. O'Dell tells many stories about the landmarks the *Arctic Star* encountered along the way. Some of those landmarks were already familiar to O'Dell's readers, especially since a chapter in the book is devoted to the Battle of San Pasqual, which is featured in *Carlota*, another of O'Dell's books.

Other landmarks are much more obscure. For example, the *Arctic Star's* visit to San Francisco prompted O'Dell to recall a visit to the city. Years before, he was invited to sign books at a San Francisco bookstore. Only 32 people came, but they were unimpressed with O'Dell's speech, and 15 books were sold. At the end of the event, a wealthy San Franciscan stepped forward to purchase the remaining 85 books, which he donated to hospitals, schools, nursing homes, and prisons.

Hall served as the navigator for the voyage. To prepare for the trip, Hall and O'Dell both took a class in navigation taught by the Coast Guard. According to O'Dell, although his wife had only a modest interest in the class, she was the only member of the class to receive a perfect score on the final exam. As for O'Dell, he flunked the test.

characters whose stories stood apart from the major events that occurred around them. Rochman explained that, "He wasn't writing the history of the 'winners,' he was writing about the people who lived out of the history books. Scott O'Dell was doing this early; writing about ordinary people whose stories were never told. I think that is really powerful."[63]

Indeed, O'Dell's books and those of his successors have helped to make historical fiction a genre worthy of other awards. More and more works of historical fiction now win other top awards, such as the Newbery Medal, which is one of the top prizes for juvenile fiction in the country. This is an important development, according to Rochman:

> I think one of the things that's happened recently is that we have noticed that historical fiction is beginning to win a lot of other major awards that aren't [ordinarily] given for historical fiction a lot of stuff which historical fiction didn't win before, it's winning now. *Kira-Kira* by Cynthia Kadohata was a Newbery Medal winner a couple of years ago. It's historical fiction."[64]

In 2006, Louise Erdrich received the Scott O'Dell Award for *The Game of Silence*, the second in a planned three-book series that chronicles the life of Omakayas, a 10-year-old Ojibwe Indian girl who undergoes a coming-of-age quest. Omakayas's tribe survives on an island in Lake Superior in 1850, and the tribe is forced to find a new home as white society invades their homeland. Hall explains that, "She wrote a book that goes back to the Indians again which would have made Scott very happy because I don't think we had a book about Indians since Elizabeth George Speare won the first award" for *The Sign of the Beaver*.[65]

Some of Hall's other favorite O'Dell Award winners are Alexandra LaFaye, the winner of the 2005 honor for her book *Worth*, and Katherine Paterson, who won in 1997 for *Jip, His Story,* as well as Avi and Karen Hesse. "Those are the ones I would point to," Hall said. "I was very impressed by Alexandra LaFaye's work. I thought, 'she writes a lot like Scott.' And then there is Katherine Paterson, Karen Hesse, and Avi. I mean, we have a lot of strong writers today."[66]

"DIGNITY OF THE HUMAN SPIRIT"

O'Dell raised issues that remain important to readers today. He began his career as a writer of historical fiction with *Island of the Blue Dolphins*, a story about protection of the environment. Now, nearly 50 years later, the threat of pollution, overdevelopment, global warming, and other problems are still a significant threat. Rochman agrees, saying "I think it's a huge political issue for young people today—those who are activists. I think it's one of the most popular issues. I think there is an enthusiasm for it."[67]

Of course, there are many other issues that remain hot topics today. Although O'Dell wrote *The Road to Damietta* as a statement against war, it continues in the Middle East, Africa, and Asia in the twenty-first century. Prejudice remains a factor in the lives of many Americans, but people have been hunted and slaughtered because of their ethnic group, religion, or race in Rwanda, Sudan, and until recently, the Balkan states of Eastern Europe. O'Dell's characters usually are able to call on their courage and intelligence to make the right choices and overcome the obstacles of life.

O'Dell explained, "With all my books, I've tried to dramatize the importance of the dignity of the human spirit. That has been my goal, and everything I have written has been written with that in mind."[68]

CHRONOLOGY

1853   Juana Maria is rescued from San Nicolas, one of the California Channel Islands.

1898   Odell Gabriel Scott is born on May 23 in Los Angeles, California; later, he changes his name to Scott O'Dell.

1918   O'Dell is inducted into the U.S. Army a month before the end of World War I; he enrolls in Occidental College, Los Angeles. He will soon drop out of Occidental and two other schools, as well.

1919   O'Dell finds a job critiquing scripts for silent movies.

1920s   O'Dell works as a cameraman, writer, and production assistant for Hollywood studios; he publishes *Representative Photoplays Analyzed*; he lives and works in Rome.

1927   O'Dell publishes his first novel for adult readers, *Woman of Spain: A Story of Old California.*

1942   O'Dell enlists in the U.S. Air Force; he is discharged from the Air Force and serves on a Coast Guard Auxiliary patrol in California.

1947   O'Dell takes a job as a book editor with the *Los Angeles Daily News*; he publishes *Hill of the Hawk.*

1948   O'Dell marries his first wife, Jane Dorsa Rattenbury; he later divorces Jane and marries Elizabeth Hall.

1953   O'Dell publishes *Man Alone* (with William Doyle).

1960   O'Dell publishes *Island of the Blue Dolphins*; he bases the story on the life of Juana Maria, the Lone Woman of San Nicolas, whose story he learned in the 1920s.

1964   Film version of *Island of the Blue Dolphins* is released, starring Celia Kaye as Karana.

1966   O'Dell publishes *The King's Fifth.*

1967   O'Dell publishes *The Black Pearl.*

1968   O'Dell publishes *The Dark Canoe,* considered a sequel to the Herman Melville classic *Moby-Dick.*

1969 O'Dell publishes *Journey to Jericho,* his first book for elementary school readers.

1970 O'Dell publishes *Sing Down the Moon,* the story of the Long Walk of the Navajo Indians.

1972 O'Dell publishes *The Treasure of Topo-el-Bampo.*

1973 O'Dell publishes *The Cruise of the Arctic Star.*

1974 Publishes *Child of Fire,* his first story about contemporary issues.

1975 O'Dell publishes *The Hawk That Dare Not Hunt by Day.*

1976 O'Dell publishes *Zia,* a sequel to *Island of the Blue Dolphins*; he also publishes *The 290.*

1977 O'Dell publishes *Carlota.*

1978 O'Dell publishes *Kathleen, Please Come Home.*

1979–1983 O'Dell publishes the Seven Serpents Trilogy: *The Captive, The Feathered Serpent,* and *The Amethyst Ring*; he also publishes *Sarah Bishop* (1980), *The Spanish Smile* (1982), and *The Castle in the Sea* (1983).

1982 O'Dell establishes Scott O'Dell Award for Historical Fiction.

1984 O'Dell publishes *Alexandra.*

1985 O'Dell publishes *The Road to Damietta.*

1986 O'Dell publishes *Streams to the River, River to the Sea,* his novel about the Lewis and Clark expedition.

1987 O'Dell publishes *The Serpent Never Sleeps.*

1988 O'Dell publishes *Black Star, Bright Dawn.*

1989 O'Dell publishes *My Name Is Not Angelica*; he dies on October 15.

1991 Elizabeth Hall completes and publishes *Thunder Rolling in the Mountains.*

NOTES

Chapter 1

1 Scott O'Dell. "My Life and Books." Available online. URL: http//:www.scottodell.com.

2 Quoted in Anne Commire, ed., *Something About the Author, vol. 60.* Detroit: Gale Research, 1990, p. 115.

3 Quoted in Scot Peacock, ed., *Contemporary Authors New Revision Series, vol. 112.* Farmington Hills, Mich.: Thomson Gale, 2003, p. 256.

Chapter 2

4 Elizabeth Hall, interview by Hal Marcovitz, August 8, 2006.

5 Quoted in David L. Russell, *Scott O'Dell.* New York: Twayne, 1999, p. 3.

6 Ibid.

7 Quoted in Simone Payment, *Scott O'Dell.* New York: Rosen, 2006, p. 20.

8 O'Dell, "My Life and Books," Available online. URL: http//:www.scottodell.com.

9 Quoted in Conrad Wesselhoeft, "'Blue Dolphins' Author Tells Why He Writes for Children," *New York Times,* April 15, 1984, p. 27.

10 Quoted in Russell, *Scott O'Dell,* p. 4.

11 Quoted in Wesselhoeft, "'Blue Dolphins' Author Tells Why He Writes for Children," p. 27.

12 *A Visit With Scott O'Dell,* Houghton Mifflin Author and Artist Series, VHS, 1983.

13 Elizabeth Hall, interview by Hal Marcovitz, August 8, 2006.

14 Ibid.

15 "How *Island of the Blue Dolphins* Came About." About Scott O'Dell. Scholastic, Inc. Available online. URL: http//:www .scholastic.com/kids/homework/ pdfs/Island_of_pt1.pdf.

Chapter 3

16 Elizabeth Hall, interview by Hal Marcovitz, August 8, 2006.

17 John Rowe Townsend, *A Sense of Story: Essays on Contemporary Writers for Children.* Philadelphia: J.B. Lippincott, 1971, p. 155.

18 Elizabeth Hall, interview by Hal Marcovitz, August 8, 2006.

19 Hazel Rochman, interview by Hal Marcovitz, August 16, 2006.

20 Quoted in Russell, *Scott O'Dell,* p. 127.

21 Townsend, *A Sense of Story: Essays on Contemporary Writers for Children,* p. 155.

22 Quoted in Peacock, ed.,
*Contemporary Authors New
Revision Series, vol. 112*, p. 256.

Chapter 4

23 "A Bittersweet Homecoming,"
Smithsonian (August 2005).
Available online. URL: http//:
www.smithsonianmagazine.com/
issues/2005/august/lewisclark
.htm.

24 *A Visit With Scott O'Dell*,
Houghton Mifflin Author and
Artist Series, VHS, 1983.

25 Quoted in Justin Wintle and
Emma Fisher, *The Pied Pipers:
Interviews With the Influential
Creators of Children's Literature.*
New York: Paddington Press,
1975, p. 176.

26 Quoted in Anne Commire, ed.,
*Something About the Author, vol.
12*. Detroit: Gale Research, 1977,
p. 163.

27 Elizabeth Hall, interview by Hal
Marcovitz, August 8, 2006.

28 Ibid.

29 Quoted in Commire, *Something
About the Author, vol. 60*, p. 118.

30 Ibid., pp. 118–119.

31 O'Dell, "My Life and Books,"
Available online. URL: http//:
www.scottodell.com.

32 Ibid.

33 Ibid.

34 Ibid.

35 *A Visit With Scott O'Dell*,
Houghton Mifflin Author and
Artist Series, VHS, 1983.

Chapter 5

36 Elizabeth Hall, interview by Hal
Marcovitz, August 8, 2006.

37 Ibid.

38 Amy Benfer, "'Girl, Revised,"
New York Times, March 6, 2004,
p. A-15.

39 Quoted in Bobbie Ann Mason,
*The Girl Sleuth: On the Trail of
Nancy Drew, Judy Bolton and
Cherry Ames*. Athens, Georgia:
University of Georgia Press,
1995, p. 53.

40 Ibid.

41 Quoted in David Halberstam, *The
Fifties*. New York: Villard Books,
1993, pp. 595–596.

42 Quoted in Commire, *Something
About the Author, vol. 60*,
p. 118.

43 *A Visit With Scott O'Dell*,
Houghton Mifflin Author and
Artist Series, VHS, 1983.

44 Elizabeth Hall, interview by Hal
Marcovitz, August 8, 2006.

Chapter 6

45 Elizabeth Hall, interview by Hal
Marcovitz, August 8, 2006.

46 Quoted in Dee Brown, *Bury
My Heart at Wounded Knee*.
New York: Bantam Books, 1970,
p. 27.

47 Quoted in Commire, *Something
About the Author, vol. 60*, p. 117.

48 Ibid.

49 Quoted in Russell, *Scott O'Dell*,
p. 71.

Chapter 7

50 Elizabeth Hall, interview by Hal Marcovitz, August 8, 2006.

51 Quoted in, Jeannine L. Laughlin and Sherry Laughlin, *Children's Authors Speak*. Englewood, Colo.: Libraries Unlimited, 1993, pp. 184–185.

52 Quoted in Russell, *Scott O'Dell*, p. 87.

53 Quoted in Peacock, *Contemporary Authors New Revision Series, vol. 112*, p. 257.

Chapter 8

54 O'Dell, "My Life and Books," Available online. URL: http//: www.scottodell.com.

55 Quoted in Russell, *Scott O'Dell*, p. 118.

56 Hazel Rochman, "The Scott O'Dell Award for Historical Fiction," *Book Links*, vol. 14, no. 1 (September 2004): pp. 40–41.

57 Hazel Rochman, interview by Hal Marcovitz, August 16, 2006.

58 Hazel Rochman, "Talking with Richard Peck." *Book Links,* vol. 14, no. 1 (September 2004): p. 45.

59 Ibid., p. 44.

60 Ibid.

61 Ibid.

62 Hazel Rochman, interview by Hal Marcovitz, August 16, 2006.

63 Ibid.

64 Ibid.

65 Elizabeth Hall, interview by Hal Marcovitz, August 8, 2006.

66 Ibid.

67 Hazel Rochman, interview by Hal Marcovitz, August 16, 2006.

68 Quoted in Laughlin and Laughlin, *Children's Authors Speak*, p. 185.

WORKS BY
SCOTT O'DELL

For Young Readers

1960 *Island of the Blue Dolphins*

1966 *The King's Fifth*

1967 *The Black Pearl*

1968 *The Dark Canoe*

1969 *Journey to Jericho*

1970 *Sing Down the Moon*

1972 *The Treasure of Topo-el-Bampo*

1973 *The Cruise of the Arctic Star*

1974 *Child of Fire*

1975 *The Hawk That Dare Not Hunt by Day*

1976 *Zia*

1976 *The 290*

1977 *Carlota*

1978 *Kathleen, Please Come Home*

1979 *The Captive*

1980 *Sarah Bishop*

1981 *The Feathered Serpent*

1982 *The Spanish Smile*

1983 *The Castle in the Sea*

1983 *The Amethyst Ring*

1984 *Alexandra*

1985 *The Road to Damietta*

1986 *Streams to the River, River to the Sea: A Novel of Sacagawea*

1987 *The Serpent Never Sleeps: A Novel of Jamestown and Pocahontas*

1988 *Black Star, Bright Dawn*

1989 *My Name Is Not Angelica*

1991 *Thunder Rolling in the Mountains* (with Elizabeth Hall)

Other

1924 *Representative Photoplays Analyzed*

1934 *Woman of Spain: A Story of Old California*

1947 *Hill of the Hawk*

1953 *Man Alone* (with William Doyle)

1957 *Country of the Sun, Southern California: An Informal History and Guide*

1958 *The Sea Is Red: A Novel*

1967 *The Psychology of Children's Art* (with Rhoda Kellogg)

POPULAR BOOKS

ISLAND OF THE BLUE DOLPHINS

Scott O'Dell's most renowned work tells the story of Karana, a young girl who survives on a deserted island for 18 years by making peace with nature and learning to live in concert with the wildlife on the island.

MY NAME IS NOT ANGELICA

Sold into slavery, Raisha is an African girl who arrives at the island of St. Thomas in the Caribbean, where her owners change her name to Angelica. Although Raisha eventually wins her freedom, the book ends tragically after an unsuccessful revolt by the slaves on the island.

THE ROAD TO DAMIETTA

Young Ricca Montanera falls in love with Francis di Barnardone, who has dedicated his life to helping the poor. Hoping to win his heart, Ricca pursues Francis as he joins the Crusades and participates in the Christian sacking of the Egyptian city of Damietta.

SING DOWN THE MOON

This book tells the sad story of the Long Walk, the forced migration of the Navajo Indians from their homeland in Arizona to a reservation in New Mexico. Bright Morning and her husband, Tall Boy, refuse to be imprisoned on the reservation and make plans to escape.

THUNDER ROLLING IN THE MOUNTAINS

Scott O'Dell's final book, which was finished by his widow Elizabeth Hall, recounts the plight of the Nez Perce Indians, who were driven from their lands in Idaho and Oregon, and forced to flee to Canada.

ZIA

Intended as a sequel to *Island of the Blue Dolphins*, the book tells the story of Karana's orphaned niece, Zia, who is living in the Santa Barbara Mission when Karana is rescued. Zia becomes involved in an uprising among the oppressed Hispanic workers at the mission.

POPULAR CHARACTERS

BRIGHT MORNING

The central character in *Sing Down the Moon*, the Navajo shepherd girl refuses to remain on the reservation. She and her husband return to their homeland in Arizona, where they begin new lives after finding the shelter of a cave.

MANUEL CASTILLO

The central figure in *Child of Fire* shows his courage by jumping into a ring to face a charging bull; later, he leaves his life as a hoodlum to help poor farm laborers win their rights.

KARANA

The central character in *Island of the Blue Dolphins*, Karana is the first of many strong and independent young women featured by O'Dell in his stories. Karana lives alone on San Nicolas Island for 18 years, surviving her ordeal by learning to respect nature.

RICCA MONTANERA

The central character in *The Road to Damietta*, Ricca falls in love with the man who would become St. Francis of Assisi; hoping to win his heart, Ricca follows Francis to the Middle East, where he participates in the Crusades.

RAISHA

The central character in *My Name Is Not Angelica*, Raisha is an African girl who is captured and sold into slavery. Throughout the story, she maintains her defiant attitude and refuses to accept the new name, Angelica, which her owners have given her.

SOUND OF RUNNING FEET

The central character in *Thunder Rolling in the Mountains*, Sound of Running Feet makes her way to Canada and finds Sitting Bull. She tries to convince the great Sioux chief to come to the aid of the Nez Perce Indians.

ZIA

The central character in *Zia*, the sequel to the *Island of the Blue Dolphins*, Karana's orphaned niece continues the story after her aunt's rescue from the island. Zia escapes from the Santa Barbara Mission to seek her homeland, accompanied by Karana's dog, Rontu-Aru.

MAJOR AWARDS

1960 *Island of the Blue Dolphins* selected for Rupert Hughes Award by the Maui Writers Conference.

1961 *Island of the Blue Dolphins* selected for the American Library Association's John Newbery Medal, the University of Wisconsin Lewis Carroll Shelf Award, and the Southern California Council on Literature for Children and Young People Notable Book Award.

1962 *Island of the Blue Dolphins* awarded the Hans Christian Andersen Award of Merit by the International Board on Books for Young People.

1963 *Island of the Blue Dolphins* awarded the William Allen White Award by Emporia State University, Kansas, as well as the German Juvenile International Award by the Federal Republic of Germany.

1964 *Island of the Blue Dolphins* awarded the Nene Award by the Hawaii Library Association.

1967 *The King's Fifth* selected as a Newbery Honor Book.

1968 *The King's Fifth* awarded the German Juvenile International Award; *The Black Pearl* selected as a Newbery Honor Book.

1970 *Sing Down the Moon* cited as a Children's Book of the Year by the Child Study Association of America.

1971 *Sing Down the Moon* named a Newbery Honor Book.

1972 O'Dell awarded the Hans Christian Andersen Medal for lifetime achievement by the International Board on Books for Young People; *The Treasure of Topo-el-Bampo* cited as a Children's Book of the Year by the Child Study Association of America.

1973 *Sing Down the Moon* awarded the Freedoms Foundation Award.

1974 *Child of Fire* cited as a Children's Book of the Year by the Child Study Association of America and selected for the *New York Times* Outstanding Book Citation.

1975 *The Hawk That Dare Not Hunt By Day* cited as a Children's Book of the Year by the Child Study Association of America.

1976 *Zia* and *The 290* cited as Children's Books of the Year by the Child Study Association of America; *Island of the Blue Dolphins,* selected among the "10 Best American Children's Books of the Past 200 Years" by the Children's Literature Association.

1978 O'Dell awarded the Regina Medal by the Catholic Library Association for his body of work.

1981 O'Dell awarded the FOCAL (Friends of Children and Literature) Award by the Los Angeles Public Library.

1984 *Sing Down the Moon* selected as a Contemporary Classic for Young Adults by *Booklist* magazine; *Alexandra,* awarded the Parents Choice Award for Literature by the Parents Choice Foundation.

1986 *Streams to the River, River to the Sea* awarded the Parents Choice Award for Literature by the Parents Choice Foundation, and the Scott O'Dell Award for Historical Fiction.

1987 *Streams to the River, River to the Sea* cited as a Children's Book of the Year by the Child Study Association of America.

1989 O'Dell awarded the School Library Media Specialist of Southeastern New York and the Northern Westchester Center for the Arts Award.

1990 *Sing Down the Moon* selected by the Children's Literature Association as a Phoenix Award Honor Book.

2000 *School Library Journal* picked *Island of the Blue Dolphins* as one of the "Books that shaped the century."

BIBLIOGRAPHY

Books

Brown, Dee. *Bury My Heart at Wounded Knee*. New York: Bantam Books, 1970.

Commire, Anne, ed. *Something About the Author, vol. 60*. Detroit: Gale Research, 1990.

———. *Something About the Author, vol. 12*. Detroit: Gale Research, 1977.

Halberstam, David. *The Fifties*. New York: Villard Books, 1993.

Laughlin, Jeannine L., and Sherry Laughlin. *Children's Authors Speak*. Englewood, Colo.: Libraries Unlimited, 1993.

Mason, Bobbie Ann. *The Girl Sleuth: On the Trail of Nancy Drew, Judy Bolton and Cherry Ames*. Athens, Georgia: University of Georgia Press, 1995.

O'Dell, Scott. *Alexandra*. New York: Ballantine Books, 1984.

———. *Black Star, Bright Dawn*. New York: Fawcett Juniper, 1988.

———. *Carlota*. Boston: Houghton Mifflin, 1977.

———. *Child of Fire*. Boston: Houghton Mifflin, 1974.

———. *Island of the Blue Dolphins*. New York: Dell Publishing, 1978.

———. *The Road to Damietta*. Boston: Houghton Mifflin, 1985.

———. *Sarah Bishop*. New York: Scholastic, 1980.

———. *The Serpent Never Sleeps*. Boston: Houghton Mifflin, 1987.

———. *Sing Down the Moon*. Boston: Houghton Mifflin, 1970.

———. *Streams to the River, River to the Sea*. New York: Fawcett Books, 1986.

———. *The 290*. Boston: Houghton Mifflin, 1976.

———. *Zia*. Boston: Houghton Mifflin, 1976.

Payment, Simone. *Scott O'Dell*. New York: Rosen, 2006.

Peacock, Scot, ed. *Contemporary Authors New Revision Series, vol. 112*. Farmington Hills, Mich.: Thomson Gale, 2003.

Russell, David L. *Scott O'Dell*. New York: Twayne, 1999.

Townsend, John Rowe. *A Sense of Story: Essays on Contemporary Writers for Children*. Philadelphia: J.B. Lippincott, 1971.

Wintle, Justin, and Emma Fisher. *The Pied Pipers: Interviews With the Influential Creators of Children's Literature*. New York: Paddington Press, 1975.

Periodicals

"A Bittersweet Homecoming." *Smithsonian* (August 2005). Available online. URL: http://www.smithsonianmagazine.com/issues/2005/august/lewisclark.htm.

Benfer, Amy. "Girl, Revised." *New York Times* (March 6, 2004): p. A-15.

Rochman, Hazel. "The Scott O'Dell Award for Historical Fiction." *Book Links*, vol. 14, no. 1, (September 2004): pp. 41–42.

———. "Talking with Richard Peck." *Book Links,* vol. 14, no. 1 (September 2004): pp. 44–45.

Strauch, Barbara. "Camping on an Island of Menacing Mice." *New York Times,* October 3, 1999, sec. 5, p. 8.

Thompson, Howard. "Island of the Blue Dolphins Has Premier." *New York Times,* July 4, 1964, p. 8.

Wesselhoeft, Conrad, "'Blue Dolphins' Author Tells Why He Writes for Children." *New York Times,* April 15, 1984, sec. 22, p. 27.

Interviews

Hall, Elizabeth. Interview by Hal Marcovitz. August 8, 2006.

Rochman, Hazel. Interview by Hal Marcovitz. August 16, 2006.

Videotape

A Visit With Scott O'Dell, Houghton Mifflin Author and Artist Series, 1983.

FURTHER READING

Ambrose, Steven E. *Undaunted Courage: Meriwether Lewis, Thomas Jefferson and the Opening of the American West*. New York: Simon and Schuster, 1996.

Carson, Rachel. *Silent Spring*. Boston: Mariner Books, 2002.

Defoe, Daniel. *Robinson Crusoe*. New York: Penguin Classics, 2003.

Melville, Herman. *Moby-Dick*. Victoria, B.C.: Castle Books, 2004.

O'Dell, Scott. *The Cruise of the Arctic Star*. Boston: Houghton Mifflin, 1973.

Scott, Sir Walter. *Ivanhoe*. New York: Penguin Classics, 2000.

Stevenson, Robert Louis. *Treasure Island*. New York: Signet Classics, 1998.

Wyss, Johann. *The Swiss Family Robinson*. New York: Signet Classics, 2004.

Web Sites

"About Scott O'Dell," Scholastic, Inc.
http://www.scholastic.com/kids/homework/pdfs/Island_of_pt1.pdf

"History of Jamestown," The Association for the Preservation of Virginia Antiquities
http://www.apva.org/history/index.html

"Island of the Blue Dolphins." San Diego Museum of Man
http://www.museumofman.org/html/education_bluedolphins.html

"The Lewis and Clark Journey of Discovery: Sacagawea"
http://www.nps.gov/archive/jeff/LewisClark2/CorpsOfDiscovery/TheOthers/Civilians/Sacagawea.htm

"The Official Site of the Iditarod"
http://www.iditarod.com/

Scott O'Dell Home Page
http://www.scottodell.com/

PICTURE CREDITS

INDEX

ABOUT THE CONTRIBUTOR

HAL MARCOVITZ is a writer based in Chalfont, Pennsylvania. His other titles in this series include biographies of Bruce Coville, R.L. Stine, Will Hobbs, Maurice Sendak, and Pat Mora.